Baking on Her Own

BAKING
ON
HER OWN

A Skill-Building Cookbook for Girls

SARAH AMORESE

Illustrations by Enya Todd

R

**ROCKRIDGE
PRESS**

For general information on our other products and services or to obtain technical support, please contact our Customer Care Department within the United States at (866) 744-2665, or outside the United States at (510) 253-0500.

Rockridge Press publishes its books in a variety of electronic and print formats. Some content that appears in print may not be available in electronic books, and vice versa.

TRADEMARKS: Rockridge Press and the Rockridge Press logo are trademarks or registered trademarks of Callisto Media Inc. and/or its affiliates, in the United States and other countries, and may not be used without written permission. All other trademarks are the property of their respective owners. Rockridge Press is not associated with any product or vendor mentioned in this book.

Interior and Cover Designer: Monica Cheng
Art Producer: Hannah Dickerson
Editor: Reina Glenn
Production Manager: Michael Kay
Production Editor: Sigi Nacson

Illustrations © 2020 Enya Todd
Author photo courtesy of C. Nathan Pulley Photography

ISBN: Print 978-1-64739-781-4
Ebook 978-1-64739-467-7
R0

*I would like to dedicate this to
my mostly adult children, Peter and Sienna.
May the joy of your creativity
flood your consciousness
and disrupt your logic often.*

Contents

Girl-Powered Baking

Welcome, baker! If you're opening this book, it means you are pursuing your baking goals, and that automatically earns you brownie points.

When I first opened my own bakery, my children were the same ages you are now. Not only did they like sneaking down to my shop in their pajamas for dessert, but they also enjoyed helping me, after school and on weekends, make what the bakery sold. Like you, they were capable of far more than just decorating holiday cookies. I have also been amazed by the kiddos in my baking classes. They might have needed a step stool to reach their workstations and some assistance removing their baked goods from the oven, but their results were *amazing*—as good as or even better than the adults standing right next to them!

Every time you bake, you will learn something new. That does not mean everything you bake will come out perfectly the first time. That rarely happens, even for experienced bakers. Baking is challenging! The most important thing is to **always try again**. We bakers are never-give-uppers! You will see that, with each new recipe you try, you will get more and more confident until every recipe in this book is a snap. Conquering the challenge is one of the most rewarding parts of baking (the other part, of course, is the delicious food!).

But, if you're ever unsure about reading a recipe or using a tool, **don't be afraid to ask for help.** Professional bakers don't do everything alone, and neither should you. Asking for help will not only keep you safe, but also make you more productive. Baking is a team sport!

Baking on Your Own

Is baking your magic power? Are you courageously curious, especially when you tie on an apron? Have your friends and family swooned over your kitchen creations? If so, lucky you! You have discovered the ability to excite and delight others with your scrumptious, finger-licking delicious food. If you're ready to take your baking and decorating skills to the next level, then come along, pastry pioneer. This book of recipes will be your guide through many new kitchen adventures. Together, we will work to expand your culinary awesomeness!

Recipe for Baking Success

TOOLS YOU'LL NEED

Your whole heart

Your caring soul

Your clever brain

Your great attitude

Your careful hands

All of your senses, especially taste!

INGREDIENTS

1 part curiosity plus 1 heaping sense of adventure

½ part knowledge (this book!)

2 parts working clean and organized

2 parts safety and asking for help when you need it

INSTRUCTIONS

1. Be safe! Handle sharp or hot items carefully.
2. Be prepared. Organize your tools and ingredients before baking.
3. Work tidy! Always clean as you go.
4. Take notes. Use the Baker's Notes at the end of most recipes to write down anything you want to remember next time you bake.
5. Never give up! You may not succeed the first time you try out a new recipe—consider that your warm-up. And remember: Most baking disasters are still delicious to eat!

Prepare, Prepare, Prepare

Preparation and Safety (P&S) are skills that every great baker needs to master. It takes both time and experience in your kitchen to fully develop your P&S skills, but if you're reading this book, you're off to a good start!

A Baker's P&S Checklist

What tool do professional bakers, firefighters, brain surgeons, and Nobel Prize–winning scientists use? A good checklist! Before you start baking, make sure you cross off every box on this list:

☐ **Is someone around to help me and to keep me safe?** Never, ever bake alone. This is what I call the **Baking Buddy System**. Always have an adult (your Baking Buddy) nearby when you bake, even if you're doing it all by yourself. Baking is risky business! Very often you will need to use sharp knives and hot ovens. Always ask for help when you need it.

☐ **Have I completely read through my recipe?** Do I understand each step? Do I have enough time to make my recipe, including not only the prep and bake times, but also the cool time?

☐ **Do I have all the ingredients to bake my recipe?** Or will I need to make a shopping list for my Baking Buddy to pick up at the grocery store?

☐ **Do I have all the tools to make my recipe?** Look through the instructions and gather all the bowls, hand tools, or appliances the recipe calls out. You'll see the tools **bolded** in every recipe.

Make Sure You Have These Common Ingredients

Before you start baking, make sure your pantry is stocked with all the essential ingredients you need to support your purpose: baking! Many of these ingredients will already be familiar to you. Flour, eggs, butter, and sugar are in nearly every recipe in this book. I call them the "backbone of baking," because, of course, they've got your back!

All-Purpose Flour: This is your "Goldilocks" of all flour—not too strong (like bread flour), not too weak (like cake flour), but just right for all the recipes in this book. It gives baked goods their structure and texture.

Baking Soda, Baking Powder, and Yeast: Also known as leaveners, these ingredients lighten and soften your batters and doughs, allowing them to grow (rise) with moisture and heat. Yeast is actually a group of teeny-tiny living organisms that eat sugar and release carbon dioxide, which is what makes dough expand!

Butter: Though it comes in many forms, all of the recipes in this book use **regular salted butter** in three different preparations: cold, softened, or melted. The way the butter is prepared in each recipe defines the butter's purpose (cold butter acts very differently from melted butter and will produce a very different finished product). Always be sure to chill, soften, or melt your butter as the recipe instructs.

Chocolate: As someone who used to run a chocolate shop, I believe the saying that "nine out of ten people love chocolate, and the tenth person is always lying" (but I'm a little biased!). For the recipes in this book, you will need chocolate as an ingredient in three ways:

Chocolate Bars: You know these! The kind you open and eat as is, without any other ingredients. You can use either milk chocolate or dark chocolate. Bar chocolate is the star ingredient in Flourless Chocolate Cake (page 104) and Dark Chocolate Truffles (page 136).

Chocolate Chips: This type of chocolate has a special type of fat added to it to keep it from completely melting in the oven (that's how chocolate chip cookies keep their chips and don't turn into chocolate puddles). These come in three forms: milk, white, and semisweet.

Cocoa Powder: This product is made by grinding up cacao beans (the main ingredient in chocolate) and removing the fat (called cocoa butter) from them. What's left over is a powder that tastes chocolaty.

Cornstarch: When used with heat and water, cornstarch helps thicken foods. For instance, if you're making a sauce and it's too runny, adding a cornstarch slurry (a mixture of cornstarch and water) and simmering the sauce for a few minutes could help thicken it to the right consistency.

Eggs: Magical eggs! What can't they do? Eggs provide structure, texture, moisture, color, and flavor to your baked goods. Eggs come in various sizes, but all of the recipes in this book use large eggs.

Granulated Sugar, Brown Sugar, and Powdered Sugar: These types of sugars provide sweetness and help crusts become golden in the oven. They all come from the same plants (sugar cane or sugar beets), but are processed differently to achieve various baking results. It is important to use the exact type of sugar called for in your recipe.

Honey, Corn Syrup, and Molasses: You can consider these ingredients liquid sugars—they do everything the dry sugars do, but they're especially great at keeping moisture in your cakes and cookies and helping your frostings become smooth and silky.

Milk and Heavy Cream: The recipes in this book use **whole milk** and **heavy cream**. That's important to know because sometimes milk is processed to reduce fat (such as with 2% and fat-free milk), which doesn't work as well in baking, but whole milk has all the fat the milk had in it when it came from the cow. Heavy cream has the highest amount of fat of any liquid dairy product. That fat is the key to making whipped cream. Remember, baking is a science!

Nonstick Cooking Spray: This is both an ingredient and an essential tool. You'll use it to grease your baking pans and keep your beautiful pastries from getting destroyed by having them stick to the pan you baked them in. You can always use butter to grease a pan, but because butter also contains water, it doesn't always work as well as nonstick cooking spray.

Nuts: These are the "seeds" of trees. They provide flavor, added nutrition, and texture to baked goods. You can purchase them whole, chopped, or sliced.

Salt: As important to baking as sugar, salt helps to balance the sweetness in any given recipe and can even amplify the flavors of other ingredients. There are many different types of salt, but regular table salt is the best choice for most baking recipes. (Fun fact: All salt comes from the sea!)

Sour Cream and Cream Cheese: Like the name says, sour cream is heavy cream that's been intentionally soured by lemon juice or bacteria (the good kind!). It's thicker than regular cream and adds rich flavor to baked goods. Cream cheese is a soft, velvety smooth, slightly tangy fresh cheese. It's what gives cheesecake its name and is also delicious in frostings and custards.

Spices, Flavorings, and Zests: As a baker, one of your missions is to pair flavors together in balanced, pleasing ways. Some flavors taste good together, and some do not. Sardines in a chocolate cake? No way! But a tiny touch of instant espresso powder in the crust of Caramelized Banana Cream Pie (page 126) complements the caramel flavors. Spices come from the seeds, bark, and roots of flavorful edible plants such as cinnamon, nutmeg, cloves, and ginger. All spices used in these recipes call for the ground form. Zest is what you get when you grate the peel of citrus fruits like lemons, limes, and oranges. Zest is just from the thin colored layer of the peel and never includes any of the bitter, spongy white part (called the pith) of the peel.

Vanilla Extract: The most common flavor enhancer used in baking, this teeny bottle of liquid comes from the long, bean-like fruit of a tropical orchid. A touch of vanilla makes everything sweet taste richer, and makes chocolate taste more chocolaty. The recipes in this book use pure (not imitation) vanilla extract.

Put Together Your Baker's Toolbox

Having the right tools makes baking easier. Knowing how to use them properly and operate them safely makes baking a triumph! You will use the following tools repeatedly in the upcoming recipes. Take good care of them. Keep them clean and organized so they're ready when you need them next. This is where the art and science of baking collide with engineering!

Baker's Uniform: Oven mitts, apron, hair tie (if you have long hair)

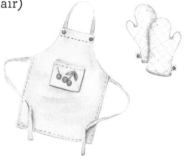

Baking Sheets (13-by-18-inch): There are lots of different sizes of baking sheets out there, but anytime you see one mentioned in this book, it's referring to this large size. You will need at least 2. Be sure they have edges (sometimes baking sheets are completely flat). The heavier and thicker the metal, the better.

Box Grater: You can use the side with the finest holes to zest citrus fruits.

Cake Pans (8 inches): Look for round pans that measure 8 inches across. You will need 2 to make a layer cake.

Food Processor: Like a blender, this appliance breaks food into small pieces, like breaking crackers into crumbs or creating a silky sauce.

Handheld Electric Mixer with Beater Attachments: This is the best tool for whipping heavy cream and egg whites to fluffy white peaks. It is also great for creaming butter and sugar together, which gives an added lift to all sorts of pastries.

Measuring Spoons and Cups: There are two types of measuring cups: the kind with a spout (for liquid ingredients like milk) and the kind with a flat top (for dry ingredients like flour).

Ladle: Use this to slowly drizzle hot ingredients into a batter without overheating it.

Melon Baller/Ice Cream Scoop: These tools are similar in that they both scoop small rounded portions—super handy for evenly measuring batters, doughs, and truffles!

Loaf Pan (5-by-9-inch): This rectangular pan is for breads and loaves that take a long time to bake. Glass is best, but metal works, too.

Mixing Bowls: Many different sizes are helpful. It is nice to have some that are plastic or glass, as these are microwave-safe.

Muffin Pans: A baking pan that has equal-size cups (usually 12) built right into it to form muffins or cupcakes. You will need 2.

Parchment Paper, Plastic Wrap, and Aluminum Foil: Use these for lining your pans and covering your baked goods.

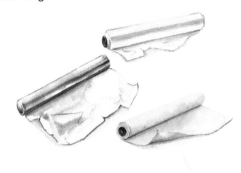

Pastry Blender: When you're making dough, you'll use this tool to *cut* butter into flour (more on this later).

Pastry Brush: A paintbrush for food! You'll use it to brush an egg wash over pastry and to grease pans. Look for one made of silicone.

Pie Plate (9 inches): Glass pie plates are best because they cook more evenly, but they can be ceramic or metal as well.

Pizza Wheel: This round blade makes cutting long straight lines a snap!

Ramekins (4 ounces): Made of either ceramic or glass, these individual ovenproof baking dishes with straight sides are used for recipes like White Chocolate Crème Brûlée (page 150). You will need 6.

Roasting Pan: Not just for roasts! You'll use a large roasting pan to create a water bath for those recipes that need a little extra care (see **Water Bath**, page 19).

Rolling Pin: An essential tool for rolling out dough.

Saucepan: Despite its name, this looks more like a small pot. You'll use it to make all kinds of sauces and fillings for your baked goods.

Sharp Knife, Butter Knife, and Cutting Board: A foundational skill in baking is learning how to safely handle a sharp knife. A cutting board can give you stability as you cut your ingredient, and help keep the cutting edge of your knife sharp. Ask for help if you're not comfortable using a sharp knife yet. You will also need a butter knife for spreading butter, jams or jellies, or other soft spreads.

Sifter: This screen-like tool allows you to catch clumps you don't want in your mixes. It also makes it easy to dust powdered sugar attractively over your finished pastries.

Spatulas: You will need three different types of spatulas for the recipes in this book: a rubber spatula for mixing or folding together ingredients, a heat-resistant spatula for stirring hot ingredients on the stove or from the oven, and a large metal spatula for moving large items like tarts. Be careful—rubber and heat-resistant spatulas look the same, but rubber will melt if it gets too hot.

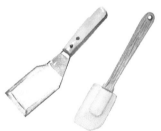

Springform Pan (9 inches): This pan has a nifty clip mechanism that lets you remove the ring around the sides without damaging your delicate cake.

Tart Pan (9 inches): This two-part pan has a removable bottom that makes it easy to take the tart out of the pan without damaging your gorgeous crust.

Whisk: A wire whisk allows for quick, smooth mixing and sometimes adds air into a mixture.

Wire Cooling Racks: When your creations emerge from the oven, you will need a safe place to set them until they cool properly. Hot pans can damage countertops.

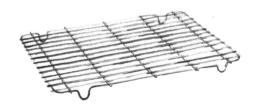

Do You Know How to Make Your Kitchen Sparkle?

By now, you understand how important staying safe in your kitchen is. Another key part to baking is working clean. Stopping periodically to clean your dishes, put things away, and wipe down your work area will help you stay focused and prevent accidents such as spills and slips.

So, do you know the most important rules about keeping clean while you bake? Quiz yourself to find out!

1. **What two ingredients look very similar, but if accidentally switched because of a disorganized workspace, would create a baked good that tasted so awful you could not eat it?**
   a. Dirt and cocoa powder
   b. Sand and sugar
   c. Sugar and salt
   d. Tomatoes and orange juice

2. **No one enjoys finding this in their food. To prevent it from making a surprise and unwelcome appearance in your delicious goodies, make sure you tie yours back or cover it. What is it?**
   a. Chocolate chips
   b. Hair
   c. Pineapple chunks
   d. Vanilla

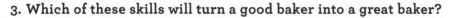

3. **Which of these skills will turn a good baker into a great baker?**

    a. Keeping an organized workspace
    b. Cleaning in-between tasks
    c. Making a list of the tools and ingredients needed before baking starts
    d. All the above

4. **It's your sister's birthday and you decide to bake her a cake at the last minute. Your only mixing bowl still has last night's popcorn in it, but you're in a hurry. Instead of washing it with soap and water, you wipe it with a paper towel. What will happen when you try to whip egg whites?**

    a. Your egg whites will not whip up into the fluffy clouds you need because there are still traces of butter in the bowl, and egg whites don't play well with fat!
    b. Your egg whites will turn into egg yolks.
    c. You will have to create a new recipe, Popcorn-Flavored Chocolate Cake.
    d. Your whites will turn blue, indicating you need to wash the bowl.

5. **After you handle one of the ingredients below, you should immediately wash your hands. Which is it and why?**

    a. Chocolate, because it is brown like dirt.
    b. Raw eggs, because they might contain bacteria that can make you sick if you eat them.
    c. Pepperoni, because it doesn't belong in dessert.
    d. Flour, because it feels funny.

Answer Key: (1) c (2) b (3) d (4) a (5) b

Master the Basics

There are certain techniques that are standard to all of baking. You will see these repeated throughout this book, so it's never too early to learn them. You will get better each and every time until you master them. Let's get to cracking and whisking!

How to Crack and Separate Eggs

Gently tap the egg against a flat surface (not the edge of a bowl) to crack the shell. Then pull the shell open and release the egg into a separate bowl from the one you're baking in (that way, if you get any shell fragments in the egg, you can remove them before they go into the batter). From there, if you need to separate the egg white from the egg yolk, use your (clean) hand to scoop up the delicate yolk and wiggle your fingers slightly to let the white run through. Always wash your hands after handling raw eggs. (Hint: Cold eggs are easier to separate than room temperature eggs.)

How to Measure Dry vs. Liquid Ingredients

To measure dry ingredients (like flour or sugar), scoop the ingredient into a flat-top measuring cup until it overflows, then use the back of a butter knife to swipe the excess off and back into the container.

To measure liquid ingredients (like milk or water), use a clear measuring cup with a spout. Get down at eye level so you can see that your liquid is right at the line on the cup where you need it to be.

How to Measure Brown Sugar

Because of its stickiness, you need to measure brown sugar differently from white sugar. Scoop it into your measuring cup or spoon and push it down with your fingers until it is packed and even with the top.

How to Measure and Soften Butter

Notice the lines on the wrapper of each stick of butter? Each one represents 1 tablespoon (and 1 stick is ½ cup). Butter is hard when it comes out of the refrigerator cold. This makes it easy to cut with a knife, but difficult to mix with other ingredients. To soften butter (meaning to bring it to room temperature), measure out the amount you need and cut it into small cubes. Spread the cubes out on a plate and let them sit for 15 to 30 minutes on your counter, until they are soft.

How to Use a Handheld Electric Mixer

This kind of mixer moves very quickly and can be dangerous, so ask an adult for help! Make sure your mixer is unplugged before putting in the beater attachments. Check that the speed setting is set to off, then plug in the mixer. Dip the beaters into the bowl with the ingredients, holding the handle securely with one hand and the bowl with the other. Switch the mixer to the lowest setting and slowly increase to the speed the recipe calls for, making sure to hold the beaters straight down into the bowl so the ingredients don't go flying out. Be especially careful with flour— it can puff up into the air if mixed on too high a speed. When finished mixing, turn the mixer off, then lift the beaters out of the bowl and immediately unplug the mixer. Be sure to keep the cord away from water.

How to Knead Dough

Kneading dough gives your baked good structure and texture. Place your dough on a clean, lightly floured countertop. You might want to stand on a stool so that you are pressing down on your dough instead of working with your arms straight out in front of you. Kneading dough is like giving it a deep massage. Scoop up the part of the dough farthest away from you with both hands and fold it over the part of the dough closest to you. Then, using the heels of your hands, push the dough down and away from you. Repeat the fold-and-push motion many times, rotating the dough 45 degrees every other push. Your dough will be ready when it is smooth and stretchy—no lumps or bumps—and you can shape it into a ball that looks like a filled water balloon.

How to Do the Toothpick Test

This test is a common way to find out whether your cake or loaf has finished baking. Insert a clean wooden toothpick into the center of your cake, then pull it out and inspect it. If the pick comes out clean or with only a few small crumbs, your baked good is done. If the pick is wet with batter, you will need to continue baking. All ovens bake differently, so you should always check for doneness even if you followed the baking time in the recipe (you may need more or less time than the recipe states).

How to Do the Beak Peaks Test

This test will help you determine if you've whipped your heavy cream or egg whites enough. After whipping, stop your mixer and dip your beaters into the mix. Pull straight up and tilt the mixer so that the beaters are horizontal. If your mixture looks like flamingos' beaks (large hooks sagging straight down from the beaters' ends), you have **soft peaks**. For **stiff peaks**, keep whipping until the mixture looks like eagles' beaks (standing out stiff from your beaters with small hooks pointing down at the ends). Here are some other helpful whip-tips: Cream must be whipped cold, and whites whip up better warm. Here's how to remember: **C**ream starts with a **C** for **Cold**, and **W**hites starts with a **W** for **Warm.**

Egg whites are very picky! They will refuse to whip up if there is a single speck of fat in the bowl or on your beaters (like a tiny bit of egg yolk, a touch of leftover cream, or a little spot of butter). You must work with exceptionally clean tools when whipping whites.

Baker's Dictionary

Now that you have entered the wonderful world of baking, you will need to learn the special language bakers use (I like to call it Bake Speak). Some of these words may already be familiar to you. However, when applied to baking, the meaning might be different. Who could have ever imagined there could be so many ways to mix things together?

These words will be *italicized* in every recipe. If you forget what they mean, turn back here for a refresher.

Beat: *(verb)* To mix ingredients together vigorously, adding air.

Blend: *(verb)* To combine and stir ingredients together until mixed well.

Blind Bake: *(verb)* To partially cook the bottom crust of a pie or tart so it doesn't become soggy from the filling.

Boil: *(noun and verb)* To cook a liquid on the stovetop until you see bubbles erupting to the surface quickly and aggressively (verb). When this happens, the liquid is boiling (noun).

Combine: *(verb)* To put ingredients together in a bowl, dish, or pan.

Cream: *(verb)* To mix butter and sugar together (most often with a hand-held electric mixer), trapping air bubbles in the butter that help batters rise in the oven.

Crimp: *(verb)* To seal the edges of a pie or tart crust shut with your fingers or a fork.

Cut in the Butter: *(verb)* To use either a large fork or pastry blender to incorporate cold butter into flour.

Divided: *(adjective)* You will see this term in an ingredient list. It means you will have 1 ingredient separated into 2 portions that will be added to the recipe at different times.

Dollop: *(noun)* A small blob of a topping like whipped cream that you scoop with a spoon and place on top of a baked good. It's often the finishing touch on a dish.

Drizzle: *(verb and noun)* To pour a very thin stream of an ingredient over another, such as drizzling icing over a cinnamon bun. The word also refers to the amount of the ingredient you're pouring (a "drizzle" of icing).

Dust: *(verb)* To lightly and evenly cover a pastry with powdered sugar or cocoa powder shaken through a sifter.

Fold: *(verb)* To gently mix ingredients with a rubber spatula by scooping down from the sides of the bowl and pulling up through the middle, then turning the spatula over to combine (and repeating until completely mixed).

Garnish: *(verb and noun)* A word that means to decorate (as a verb) or the decorations themselves (as a noun).

Generously: *(adverb)* A way of adding or spreading a large amount of an ingredient onto a surface.

Grease: *(verb)* To apply a fat, either butter or nonstick cooking spray, to cover the inside of your baking pans before you fill them. It helps you easily remove finished baked goods from your pans.

Knead: *(verb)* To mix a stiff dough together with your hands. For more detail, see **How to Knead Dough** (page 15).

Sacrifice: *(verb and noun)* To incorporate whipped cream or eggs into a batter for a fluffy texture. To do this, scoop out a small portion of the whipped egg whites or cream (the recipe will tell you how much) and mix that vigorously into your batter. Then, scoop the rest of the whipped ingredient on top of your batter and gently fold it in. The first portion you scoop in is also called the sacrifice.

Set: *(verb)* To let an ingredient or mixture rest in order to firm up (this can happen in the oven, on the countertop, or in the fridge).

Shaggy: *(adjective)* A way to describe a dough that is mixed but still clumpy. It may look like a mess, and that's okay! It is an important stage in certain baked goods that you will learn to recognize.

Sift: *(verb)* To pour a dry ingredient like powdered sugar into a sifter and shake it through to either remove clumps or decorate a finished baked good.

Simmer: *(noun)* When bubbles are gently rising to the surface of a liquid that is cooking on the stovetop.

Soft Peaks or **Stiff Peaks:** *(nouns)* These terms apply to whipping heavy cream and egg whites. To whip to the proper consistency, see **How to Do the Beak Peaks Test** (page 16).

Temper: *(verb)* To slowly bring separate ingredients of different temperatures and textures together. In this book, it refers specifically to slowly incorporating hot cream or milk into cold egg yolks to prevent the eggs from scrambling and creating unpleasant bits of hard-cooked yolks.

Toss: *(verb)* To lightly pick ingredients up and drop them gently back into the mixture to distribute a coating (like mixing fruit with sugar).

Water Bath: *(noun)* A baking method that adds more moisture to your oven and helps distribute heat for gentle baking. You create a water bath by placing the pan with your batter in a larger pan and filling the outside pan with hot tap water (making sure not to get any water into your batter).

Whip: *(verb)* To mix extremely quickly, often with a handheld electric mixer, adding enough air to an ingredient (like egg whites or heavy cream) so it becomes firm and increases in volume, forming peaks (see **Soft Peaks or Stiff Peaks,** above). Learn how to whip correctly using the Beak Peaks Test (see page 16).

Whisk: *(verb)* To quickly stir ingredients together with a fork or whisk to add air and make a mixture fluffy.

Zest: *(verb)* To use a grater to remove the very thin outside layer from the peel of a citrus fruit.

Ready, Set, Bake!

Pastry pioneer, are you ready for some whisk-y business? Let's recap a couple of things before we get started. 1) Preparation and safety—make your lists, check them twice, and ask for help when you need it. 2) Always work clean and organized. 3) Have fun! If something doesn't turn out perfectly the first time you bake it, try it again!

Recipe Guide

Prep/bake/cool times: How much time it will take to make the recipe from start to finish. "Prep" is short for "preparation" and includes the time it takes to mix, measure, chill, and otherwise get your recipe ready to bake. "Bake" is the time the recipe is actually in the oven. "Cool" is the time after baking before your recipe is ready to eat.

Yield: How big your baked good will be **or how many** servings it will make.

 Overnight icon: This icon means the recipe takes a long time and **should be split between two days**.

Difficulty icons: These icons tell you right away **how challenging** your recipe will be:

  These recipes don't have too many steps, won't take too long to put together, and shouldn't be a problem for you to make all on your own.

These recipes are a little more challenging, but nothing you can't handle with a little help. They might have tools or ingredients you have not used before, but it's exciting to learn new things!

 These recipes will be the most challenging for you. Save them for when you've got plenty of time and are ready to learn a lot!

How to Read the Recipes

A recipe is just a list of ingredients and instructions. How *you* put it together is the magic of *your* baking. But if you're ever unsure what a recipe in this book is trying to tell you, use the helpful guide below.

Ingredients: A list of every ingredient you will need to make the recipe, and how much of it. It will also say if an ingredient needs special preparation (like softened butter). Sometimes the ingredients will be split into two different sections (like a cake and its frosting), and they will be labeled for which section is which. When the instructions say something like "combine the frosting ingredients," that means you should look at the ingredient section labeled "For the frosting."

Instructions: This is the step-by-step process of making the recipe. The beginning of each step has **boldface words** to help you see what's coming. When you see an *italicized* word in the instructions, turn back to the Baker's Dictionary (page 17) for the definition, if necessary. And all of the tools you will need to make the recipe are set in **boldface. Always read through your entire recipe before you start.** This will allow you to better plan out your tasks and time.

Caution icon: This symbol means you need to be **very** careful. Baking can be dangerous—knives are sharp, ovens are hot, and electric mixers can hurt you. **When you see this icon, you may want to ask for help.**

Tips: This asterisk means there's extra information in the margins of the page to help you make your recipe a success.

Test Your Skills Challenges

This book is meant to help you become a super baker, but to really improve your skills, you will need to try some recipes that are difficult. That's why the last one or two recipes in every chapter of this book are **Test Your Skills Challenges.** These recipes may be frustrating the first time you try them, but with practice and perseverance, you will learn new baking techniques and increase your confidence.

Raise your whisk and repeat after me:

TEST YOUR SKILLS

I am a baker and I am strong.

I will not get discouraged
if a recipe seems too hard for me
the first time I bake it.

I promise to continue practicing
and developing my baking skills.

I know that I am bigger
than any recipe.

I will bake it until I make it!

Baking for Breakfast

Oh My Gran(Oh!)la

Prep time:
30 minutes

Bake time:
40 minutes

Cool time:
20 minutes

Yield:
8 cups

Ingredients

Nonstick cooking spray

½ cup (1 stick) butter

4 cups rolled oats

¾ cup assorted raw nuts (try almonds, pecans, macadamias, or pistachios)

½ cup raw hulled seeds (try pumpkin, sunflower, or sesame)

½ cup sweetened shredded coconut

1 cup packed brown sugar

½ cup maple syrup

½ cup vegetable oil

¾ cup pasteurized egg whites (from a 1-pint carton)

2 teaspoons salt

2 tablespoons unsweetened cocoa powder

1 teaspoon ground cinnamon

½ teaspoon ground nutmeg

1 cup assorted **dried fruits*** (try cranberries, cherries, strawberries, blueberries, apricots, raisins, papayas, or mangos)

1 teaspoon grated lemon zest

*If you choose larger pieces of fruit, chop them into bite-size pieces.

Instructions

1. **Preheat the oven to 325°F and prepare the baking sheets.** Before turning the oven on, adjust 2 oven racks to the middle-most positions in the oven—not too close to the top or bottom. Coat **2 baking sheets** with nonstick cooking spray.

2. **Start mixing the ingredients.** Place the butter in a **small microwave-safe bowl**, and heat in the microwave for 1 minute, until melted. In a **large mixing bowl**, *combine* the oats, nuts, seeds, coconut, brown sugar, maple syrup, vegetable oil, and melted butter and use your hands to *toss* them together.

3. **Whip the egg whites.** In a **medium mixing bowl**, use a **whisk** to *whisk* the egg whites for about 1 minute, until they are foamy. Add the salt, cocoa powder, cinnamon, and nutmeg and whisk again until everything is combined. Pour the egg mixture over the oat mixture in the large bowl and, using your hands, thoroughly mix everything together. Wash your hands thoroughly with soap and water.*

*Remember, raw eggs can carry bacteria that can make you sick if you eat it, so always wash your hands after touching them.

continues

4. **Prepare the granola and bake.** Divide the mixture between the prepared baking sheets and spread it out evenly with a **rubber spatula.** Put the sheets in the oven ⚠ and bake for 20 minutes. While the granola is baking, wash the large mixing bowl (you're going to use it again).

5. **Stir the granola.** Using **oven mitts**, remove the baking sheets from the oven ⚠ and stir very well with a **heat-resistant spatula.** Return the sheets to the oven, but this time, place the sheet that was previously on top on the bottom rack and the other on top, and rotate both sheets from front to back so the opposite sides are facing you. Continue baking for another 10 minutes. Open the oven and, using the oven mitts, rotate the sheets front to back again ⚠ and continue baking for 10 minutes more. The granola is done when it's golden brown and deliciously fragrant! Remove the sheets from the oven ⚠ and place them on a **wire cooling rack** to cool for 20 minutes.

*You can also add mini chocolate chips to this recipe, but if you do, wait to mix them in until the granola is completely cooled. Otherwise, they might melt.

6. **Add the dried fruit.** Pour the granola back into the large clean bowl and sprinkle the dried fruits* and lemon zest over the top (you may need to separate the sticky fruits with your hands). Mix the granola with the heat-resistant spatula until thoroughly combined, then enjoy!

Baker's Notes

What went well? How can you improve next time?

RECIPE: ....

NOTES: ....

....

....

....

....

....

....

....

....

....

....

....

....

Candied Bacon and Creamed Eggs

Prep time:
15 minutes

Bake time:
40 minutes

Yield:
4 servings
*(3 to 4 pieces of
bacon and
1 egg each)*

Ingredients

Nonstick cooking spray

¾ cup packed brown sugar

1 pound thick-sliced bacon

1 tablespoon butter, softened

4 tablespoons heavy cream

⅛ teaspoon salt

⅛ teaspoon pepper

4 large eggs

Instructions

1. **Preheat the oven to 350°F and prepare your work space and baking sheet.**
   Before turning the oven on, adjust an oven rack to the upper-middle position.
   Place a large piece of **parchment paper** on your counter. Cover a **baking sheet**
   with **aluminum foil**, making sure the foil wraps up the inside edges. Lightly
   spray the foil with nonstick cooking spray.

2. **Prepare the bacon.** Sprinkle ½ cup of brown sugar evenly onto the prepared baking sheet. Spread out the bacon slices on top of the brown sugar. Sprinkle the remaining ¼ cup of brown sugar over the top of the bacon.

3. **Bake the bacon for 22 to 24 minutes.** Transfer the baking sheet to the oven and bake for 8 minutes. Then, open the oven and, using tongs,* flip the bacon slices over. ⚠ Using **oven mitts**, rotate the baking sheet from front to back and continue baking for 8 more minutes. Open the oven and flip the bacon one more time* ⚠ and bake for an additional 6 to 8 minutes, until the bacon is a dark golden color, caramelly-crisp, and shiny. Using the oven mitts, remove from the oven ⚠ and, using the tongs, transfer each strip of bacon to the parchment paper to cool while you continue the recipe. Do not allow any pieces to touch. (Leave the oven on.)

    *This tool looks like a big set of pincers. It's best for grabbing and turning food that is too hot to touch with your hands.

    *Most ovens bake unevenly. The bacon slices on the outside of the sheet may bake faster than those in the middle, so rearrange the slices if you need to.

4. **Prepare the ramekins.** Using your fingers, rub the butter all over the insides of **4 ramekins**. Pour 1 tablespoon of cream into each ramekin. Add a little pinch each of salt and pepper to the cream in each ramekin.

5. **Crack the eggs.** Carefully crack one egg into each ramekin. Try not to break the yolks. Place the ramekins on **another baking sheet**, and put the sheet in the oven. ⚠

6. **Bake the eggs to your liking.** If you prefer soft yolks, bake for 10 to 12 minutes. If you like firm yolks, bake for 14 to 16 minutes. Using oven mitts, remove the pan from the oven and place each ramekin on a **serving plate**. ⚠ Serve immediately with the candied bacon.*

    *Try dipping the candied bacon into the egg yolks. Yummalicious!

Crumble Top YumYam Breakfast Muffins

Prep time:
30 minutes

Bake time:
25 minutes

Cool time:
20 minutes

Yield:
12 muffins

Ingredients

For the crumble topping

¾ cup all-purpose flour

½ cup packed brown sugar

⅛ teaspoon salt

¼ teaspoon ground cinnamon

6 tablespoons cold butter

½ cup mini marshmallows

1 tablespoon water

½ cup chopped pecans (optional)

Ingredients continued

For the muffins

Nonstick cooking spray

2¼ cups all-purpose flour

2 teaspoons baking soda

1 teaspoon baking powder

1 teaspoon salt

1 teaspoon ground cinnamon

½ teaspoon ground ginger

½ cup (1 stick) butter, **softened***

1¼ cups packed brown sugar

3 large eggs

1 large egg yolk*

1 (29-ounce) can cut **candied yams*** in light syrup

½ cup orange juice

*Turn to page 15 to learn how to soften butter.

*Turn to page 14 to learn how to separate eggs.

*If you want to use fresh yams, you'll need to first bake them at 350°F for 1 hour. When they're cool, peel and chop them into large pieces.

Instructions

1. **Preheat the oven to 350°F and prepare the muffin pan.** Before turning the oven on, adjust an oven rack to the middle position. Coat the cups of a **12-cup muffin pan** with nonstick cooking spray, or fill each cup with a **cupcake liner**.

2. **Make the crumble topping.** In a **medium mixing bowl**, *combine* the flour, brown sugar, salt, and cinnamon. Using a **butter knife**, cut the butter into small cubes and sprinkle them into the flour mixture. Using your fingers, rub the mixture

continues

together until large clumps form. In a **small bowl**, sprinkle the marshmallows with the water and *toss* to moisten, then add them to the crumble mixture along with the pecans (if you're using them). Use your fingers to toss everything together. Set the bowl aside.

3. **Sift the dry ingredients together for the muffins.** Set a **sifter** over a **medium mixing bowl** and *sift* together the flour, baking soda, baking powder, salt, cinnamon, and ginger. Set the bowl aside.

4. **Cream the butter and sugar together.** In a **large mixing bowl**, use a **handheld electric mixer** set on medium speed ⚠ to *cream* the butter and brown sugar together for about 3 minutes, until they are light and fluffy.

5. **Add the eggs.** One at a time, add the whole eggs and egg yolk to the butter mixture. Be sure to *beat* the mixture after each egg you add. Open the can of yams with a **can opener** and drain the liquid into the sink (you won't need it). Add the yams to the butter mixture and continue to beat for 30 seconds to break up the chunks. The batter will be lumpy-bumpy, and that's okay!

6. **Combine the dry ingredients with the yam mixture.** Use a **rubber spatula** to gently *fold* the flour mixture into the yam batter until thoroughly combined. Then, add the orange juice and continue to gently fold until the juice is incorporated.

7. **Spoon the batter into the prepared muffin cups.** Use a **spoon** to fill each cup about three-quarters full. Sprinkle some of the crumble topping over each muffin, making sure each one has 3 to 4 marshmallows. Place the pan in the oven. ⚠

8. **Bake the muffins for 25 minutes.** The muffins are done when they are golden brown and pass the **Toothpick Test** (see page 16). Using **oven mitts**, remove the pan from the oven ⚠ and set it on a **wire cooling rack** to cool for 20 minutes. Serve while the muffins are warm.

Baker's Notes

What went well? How can you improve next time?

RECIPE: ....

NOTES: ....

....

....

....

....

....

....

....

....

....

....

....

....

....

Cinna-Bread Pudding in a Mug

Prep time:
30 minutes

Bake time:
55 minutes

Cool time:
15 minutes

Yield:
4 large mugs

Ingredients

3 tablespoons butter, *divided*

3 to 4 leftover Sleepover Cinnamon Buns (page 44) or store-bought cinnamon rolls

1 tablespoon granulated sugar

¾ cup packed brown sugar

7 large egg yolks*

¾ teaspoon salt

1¼ teaspoons instant espresso powder

1½ tablespoons vanilla extract

2 cups plus 2 tablespoons heavy cream

2 cups plus 2 tablespoons whole milk

*Turn to page 14 to learn how to separate eggs.

Instructions

1. **Preheat the oven to 350°F and prepare the mugs.** Before turning the oven on, adjust an oven rack to the middle position. Using your fingers, rub 1 tablespoon of butter all over the insides of **4 large ceramic mugs (like a ceramic coffee mug)**.

2. **Prepare the cinnamon rolls.** Using a **sharp knife** ⚠ , cut the cinnamon rolls into small cubes. You'll need 6 to 7 cups of cubes. Include everything your rolls might have in them—nuts, fruits, glaze—it's all extra yumminess! Then, in a **small bowl**, *combine* the granulated sugar and 1 tablespoon of brown sugar. Set the bowl aside.

3. **Toast the cubes for 12 to 15 minutes.** Spread the cubes out on a **baking sheet** and place it in the oven to toast. ⚠ After 4 to 5 minutes, using **oven mitts**, take the sheet out and stir the cubes with a **heat-resistant spatula**. Return the sheet to the oven ⚠ and bake for another 4 to 5 minutes. Using the oven mitts, take the sheet out again, stir the cubes one more time, then return them to the oven ⚠ for another 4 to 5 minutes, until they are golden brown. (Watch closely to make sure they don't burn!) Using the oven mitts, remove the cubes from the oven. ⚠ Set the pan on a **wire cooling rack** to cool for 15 minutes while you continue the recipe. Wipe off your baking sheet and lower the oven temperature to 325°F.

4. **Make the filling.** In a **large mixing bowl**, use a **whisk** to *whisk* the egg yolks together. Add the remaining ¾ cup of brown sugar, the salt, instant espresso, and vanilla and whisk until combined. Pour the heavy cream into the yolk mixture and whisk until the sugar and espresso are dissolved. Add the milk and whisk until thoroughly combined.

continues

5. **Add the toasted cubes.** With a **measuring cup**, measure out 1½ cups of the toasted cubes and set them aside. Add the remaining toasted cubes to the egg mixture and stir with a **spoon**, pushing any floating pieces down into the liquid. Let it sit for 30 minutes.

*If you're a cinna–holic, sprinkle an additional ½ teaspoon cinnamon over the sugar.

6. **Fill the mugs.** With a **large spoon**, spoon the filling equally into the buttered mugs, leaving 1 inch of space at the top of the mugs. Put the toasted cubes you set aside on top of each mug, pushing them into the liquid but not completely submerging them. Place the remaining 2 tablespoons of butter in a **small microwave-safe bowl** and heat in the microwave for 30 seconds or until melted. Dip a **pastry brush** into the melted butter, brush the tops of the cubes *generously*, then sprinkle them with the mixed sugars* you set aside. Place the mugs on the clean baking sheet and place it in the oven. ⚠

*Turn this breakfast recipe into dessert by serving these bread puddings with vanilla ice cream!

7. **Bake for 35 to 40 minutes.** The bread pudding is done when the filling has risen up the sides of the mug and is bulging a little. Remove the mugs from the oven ⚠ and place them on the wire cooling rack to cool for 15 minutes before serving.*

Baker's Notes

What went well? How can you improve next time?

RECIPE: ....

NOTES: ....

....

....

....

....

....

....

....

....

....

....

....

Crunchy Monte Cristo Sandwiches

Prep time:
30 minutes

Bake time:
20 minutes

Yield:
4 servings
(2 pieces each)

Ingredients

6 slices of your favorite sandwich bread

Butter

Blackberry or raspberry jam

½ cup sour cream

½ cup shredded Swiss cheese

½ cup shredded mozzarella cheese

4 slices deli ham or turkey

½ cup all-purpose flour

2 large eggs

⅛ teaspoon salt

1½ cups panko bread crumbs or
   crushed cornflakes cereal

¼ cup vegetable oil

Powdered sugar, for *garnish*

Fresh blackberries or raspberries
   (optional), for *garnish*

Instructions

1. **Prepare the toast.** Using a **toaster** or **toaster oven,** toast the bread slices until they are golden brown. When they are cool enough to touch ⚠ , use a **butter knife** to spread butter on 1 side of 4 of the slices. Spread jam on 1 side of the remaining 2 slices.

2. **Assemble the sandwiches**

   a. Place the 4 buttered toast slices (butter-side down) on a **cutting board.**

   b. Use the butter knife to spread a little of the sour cream onto the top of each slice.

   c. Divide the shredded Swiss and mozzarella cheeses equally on top of 2 slices.

   d. Place the jam toast slices (jam-side up) on top of the cheese.

   e. Lay 2 slices of the deli ham or turkey on top of each jammy toast.

   f. Place the remaining 2 toast slices, sour cream–side down, on top of the meat. You will have 2 stacked sandwiches.

   g. Place a piece of **plastic wrap** on top of each sandwich and press down firmly with your hand to ensure everything sticks together well. Wrap the sandwiches in plastic wrap and place them in the freezer while you prepare your batter station.

3. **Preheat the oven to 425°F.** Before turning the oven on, adjust an oven rack to the upper-middle position and place a **baking sheet** in the empty oven to heat up.*

4. **Prepare your 3-step batter station.** Place the flour in a **shallow dish (like a pie plate).** Crack the eggs into a **second shallow dish**, add the salt, and *beat* the eggs with a **fork.** Place the panko bread crumbs in

*Why does the baking sheet need to be hot? Because it heats up the oil. Hot oil makes these sandwiches fry up and become crispy–cold oil would make them soggy and spongy.

continues

a **third shallow dish**. Make sure the dishes are lined up on your counter in this order: flour, eggs, bread crumbs. Place a **large plate** at the end of the line.

5. **Cut the sandwiches.** Remove the sandwiches from the freezer, unwrap them, and place them on the cutting board. Using a **sharp knife** ⚠ , carefully cut each sandwich in half diagonally, then in half again along the opposite diagonal. Each sandwich should give you 4 triangular` pieces, 8 pieces total.

6. **Cover the sandwiches with flour, egg, and bread crumbs.** Working with one triangle piece at a time, use your hands to roll the triangle in flour until it's completely covered, then shake off the excess. Dip the triangle into the egg, making sure to coat all sides, and let the excess egg drip off. Transfer the triangle to the bread crumbs and roll it around, pressing as you go to stick on a thick layer of crumbs. Place the finished triangle on the plate. Repeat this process with the remaining triangle sandwich pieces.

7. **Bake the sandwiches for 18 to 20 minutes.** Using **oven mitts**, remove the hot baking sheet from the oven ⚠ and carefully pour the oil onto the center, tilting the baking sheet every which way to coat the surface evenly. Place the sandwich pieces on the baking sheet and put them in the oven ⚠ . Bake for 9 to 10 minutes, then open the oven ⚠ and use **tongs** to flip the pieces over. Continue baking for another 9 to 10 minutes, until the triangles are golden brown. Using the oven mitts, remove from the oven ⚠ and transfer to the large plate.

8. **Serve the sandwiches.** *Dust* the triangles with powdered sugar and *garnish* with fresh berries if you like. Eat immediately (but be careful of the very hot cheese!).

Baker's Notes

What went well? How can you improve next time?

RECIPE: ....

NOTES: ....

....

....

....

....

....

....

....

....

....

....

Sleepover Cinnamon Buns

Prep time:
3 hours,
30 minutes

Bake time:
25 minutes

Cool time:
5 minutes

Yield:
12 buns

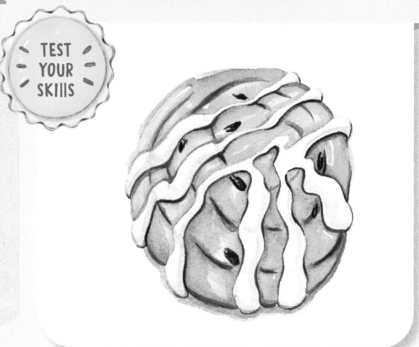

Heads up, baker: This recipe takes time. I suggest you split
it into two days. On day 1, complete steps 1 through 5. Line a
baking sheet with parchment paper and coat it with nonstick
cooking spray. After you punch your dough down, place it on the
baking sheet. Press the dough down with your hands to about
1/2 inch thick. Wrap the whole thing up loosely in a large, clean
plastic bag and press out the air. Refrigerate it overnight, then
on day 2, begin with step 6. Cover your filling and glaze with
plastic wrap, too, but no need to refrigerate these.

Ingredients

For the dough

1½ cups whole milk

⅓ cup granulated sugar

4½ teaspoons active dry yeast
(two ¼-ounce packets)

¾ cup (1½ sticks) butter

1 large egg

1 large egg yolk*

2 teaspoons vanilla extract

½ teaspoon grated lemon zest

2 teaspoons salt

4½ cups all-purpose flour, *divided,*
plus more for kneading the dough

*Turn to page 14 to learn
how to separate eggs.

For the filling

3 tablespoons butter, softened

½ cup packed brown sugar

4 teaspoons ground cinnamon

1 tablespoon all-purpose flour

1 cup raisins, dried cherries, or chopped
nuts (optional)

For the glaze

2 tablespoon whole milk

1 teaspoon vanilla extract

1 tablespoon corn syrup

⅛ teaspoon salt

1¼ cups powdered sugar

continues

Instructions

1. **Start the dough.** Pour the milk and granulated sugar in a **small microwave-safe bowl**. Microwave for 1 minute, then stir in the yeast with a **spoon** and let it sit for 10 minutes. Meanwhile, place the butter in a **separate small microwave-safe bowl** and microwave for 1 minute or until melted. Let it sit for 5 minutes to cool. In a **medium mixing bowl**, *combine* the melted butter, whole egg, egg yolk, vanilla, lemon zest, and salt, and use a **whisk** to *whisk* them together. Set the bowl aside.

*Turn to page 15 to learn how to knead dough.

2. **Mix the wet and dry ingredients together.** *Dust* a clean countertop with flour. In a **large mixing bowl**, *combine* the yeast mixture with 3 cups of flour, and mix with a **rubber spatula** for 1 minute. Then, pour in the butter mixture and stir for 1 more minute. When it starts to look like dough, transfer the dough to the floured countertop and use your hands to start to knead.* It will be very sticky at first.

*Get a step stool to stand on if the counter is too high—this will let you lean into the dough and use your weight to help you knead. (You're bigger than that dough!) If your arms get tired, ask for help.

3. **Knead the dough.** Sprinkle the dough with ½ cup of flour and *knead* it in with both hands for 3 minutes.* Add another ½ cup of flour and knead for 3 more minutes. Add the last ½ cup of flour and knead for 3 to 5 minutes, until the dough is super smooth and looks like an overfilled water balloon. Shape the dough into a ball and return it to the bowl. Cover it tightly with **plastic wrap** and let it sit in a warm area in your kitchen for about 1 hour, until it doubles in size.

4. **Meanwhile, make the filling and glaze.** In a **small bowl**, *combine* the butter, brown sugar, cinnamon, and flour and stir with a **fork** until it's fully mixed. Set the bowl aside. If you are using dried fruit or nuts, combine them in a **separate small bowl**. Set the bowl aside. In **another small bowl**, *whisk* together all the glaze ingredients until they're smooth and shiny. Cover the bowl tightly with plastic wrap and set it aside, too.

5. **Let the dough rise a second time.** After 1 hour, unwrap the dough and gently push your fist into the middle once. This removes some of the air that the dough has gained from rising. Reshape the dough into a ball, and cover the bowl again with the same piece of plastic wrap. Place the bowl back in the warm spot and let the dough rise for another 45 minutes. When the dough is almost ready, clear off a clean countertop and *dust* it with flour.

6. **Roll out the dough.** Place the dough on the floured surface and rub a **rolling pin** with a little flour. Roll out the dough, starting from the middle and using short strokes in all directions. You are aiming for a rectangle that is about 12 by 16 inches.

7. **Spread the filling on the dough.** Fill a **small bowl** with water from the sink, and set it nearby. Set the rectangle of dough the long way, so a long side is facing you. Use your hands to spread the filling evenly over the dough, leaving a 1-inch border on the long side farthest from you. If you are adding dried fruit or nuts, sprinkle them over the filling. Starting with the long side closest to you, carefully roll the dough toward the opposite side, making a long, tight log. Wet your fingers with the water from the bowl, and pinch along the seam of the dough to seal in the filling.

continues

* "Score" means to cut an indentation that doesn't go all the way through the dough. To make sure your rolls are of equal size, start by scoring the log into 3 equal parts. Then, make a score in the center of each of the 3 parts to create 6 sections. Finally, score each of the 6 sections in the center again. This will give you 12 even rolls. Now you can cut the rolls all the way through, following the marks you've already made.

8. **Cut the rolls.** Using a **sharp knife** ⚠, lightly score* the log into 12 rolls, then cut through the dough to separate the 12 rolls. Cover **2 baking sheets** with **parchment paper**, and place 6 rolls on each one with the swirl facing up, leaving plenty of space in between. Cover the pans with plastic wrap, and let the rolls rise in a warm place (again!) for 45 minutes. The rolls will get bigger but may not completely double in size. When the 45 minutes is almost up, preheat the oven to 375°F. Before turning on the oven, adjust 2 oven racks to the middle-most positions in the oven—not too close to the top or bottom.

9. **Bake the rolls (finally!).** Remove the plastic wrap from the baking sheets, and place the baking sheets in the oven. ⚠ Bake for 20 to 25 minutes, until the tops of the rolls are deep golden brown. Using **oven mitts**, remove from the oven ⚠ and let cool on a **wire cooling rack** for 5 minutes.

10. **Serve!** Using a **spoon**, *drizzle* the glaze all over the rolls, and serve immediately.

Baker's Notes

What went well? How can you improve next time?

RECIPE: ....

NOTES: ....

....

....

....

....

....

....

....

....

....

....

....

Cookies, Brownies, and Bars

Nutty Lacies

Prep time:
20 minutes

Bake time:
12 minutes
per batch

Cool time:
30 minutes
per batch

Yield: 24 cookies
(or 12 cookie
sandwiches)

Ingredients

Nonstick cooking spray

¾ cup whole raw nuts of your choice

½ cup sugar

1 slightly **heaping** tablespoon
all-purpose flour

1 tablespoon cornstarch

¼ teaspoon salt

3 tablespoons butter

1 tablespoon heavy cream

2 tablespoons corn syrup

½ teaspoon vanilla extract

*This means the flour is not
leveled off in the measuring
spoon and is mounded up
just a little bit in the center

Instructions

1. **Preheat the oven to 325°F and prepare the baking sheets.** Before turning on the oven, adjust 2 oven racks to the middle-most positions in the oven—not too close to the top or bottom. Line **3 baking sheets** with **parchment paper** and coat the parchment with nonstick cooking spray.

2. **Crush the nuts.** Place the nuts in a **large plastic bag**, then seal the bag and place it on the counter between **2 kitchen towels.** Using a **rolling pin**, gently pound and roll until the nuts are crushed into very small pieces. Transfer the crushed nuts to a **medium mixing bowl**, add the sugar, flour, cornstarch, and salt, and mix with a **small spoon** until combined. Make a crater in the middle with your fist.

3. **Mix the liquid ingredients.** In a **small microwave-safe bowl**, *combine* the butter, cream, corn syrup, and vanilla. Microwave for 1 minute or until melted, then stir with a **fork** to combine. Pour the melted butter mixture into the crater of crushed nuts in the bowl, and mix with the fork until it's fully combined. The batter will be thick, but not stiff.

4. **Portion the cookies onto the baking sheets.** Using the small spoon, scoop the batter onto the baking sheets in portions the size of a large grape. These cookies will spread a lot, so place only 8 or 9 cookies on each sheet with 3 to 4 inches of room between them. Make sure they're a few inches from the edges of the baking sheets, too. Place two of the baking sheets in the oven. ⚠

5. **Bake the cookies for 12 minutes.** You'll know they're done baking when they are a deep golden brown. Using **oven mitts**, remove the cookies from the oven ⚠ and place the pans on a **wire cooling rack** to cool for 20 to 30 minutes, until the cookies are completely cool.

continues

6. **Bake more batches.** While the first batch is cooling, repeat step 5 with the remaining dough.

7. **Serve.** Carefully remove the delicate cookies from the sheet with your hands after they're cool and enjoy!

You can also make these into cookie sandwiches! After you've turned the oven off (but while it is still warm), pour ½ cup chocolate chips into a shallow baking dish (like a pie plate). Place it in the warm oven ⚠ for 5 to 10 minutes, until the chocolate is melted but not hot. Using your hands, carefully dip the bottom side of a cookie into the chocolate and immediately stick it together with the bottom of another cookie to form a sandwich. Repeat with the remaining cookies.

Baker's Notes

What went well? How can you improve next time?

RECIPE: ....

NOTES: ....

....

....

....

....

....

....

....

....

....

....

....

Ginger Orange Spice Crinkles

Prep time:
30 minutes

Bake time:
15 minutes
per batch

Cool time:
20 minutes
per batch

Yield:
20 to 24
cookies

Ingredients

For the crinkle coating

2 large oranges

½ cup sugar

For the dough

Nonstick cooking spray

1¾ cups all-purpose flour

1 tablespoon unsweetened cocoa powder

1¼ teaspoons baking soda

½ teaspoon salt

2½ teaspoons ground ginger

½ teaspoon ground cinnamon

⅛ teaspoon ground allspice

⅛ teaspoon ground nutmeg

⅛ teaspoon ground cloves

Ingredients continued

1 large egg

1 large egg yolk*

⅓ cup molasses

½ teaspoon vanilla extract

¾ cup (1½ sticks) butter, **softened***

¾ cup packed brown sugar

*Turn to page 14 to learn how to separate eggs.

*Turn to page 15 to learn how to soften butter.

Instructions

1. **Preheat the oven to 325°F and prepare the baking sheets.** Before turning on the oven, adjust 2 oven racks to the middle-most positions in the oven—not too close to the top or bottom. Line **3 baking sheets** with **parchment paper**. Coat the parchment with nonstick cooking spray.

2. **Make the crinkle coating.** Using the smallest holes on a **box grater** (or a **Microplane zester** if you have one) ⚠ , *zest* the oranges onto a **small plate**. Add the sugar to the plate and stir carefully with a **fork** until fully mixed.

3. **Prepare the dry and wet ingredients for the dough.** In a **medium mixing bowl**, *combine* the flour, cocoa powder, baking soda, salt, ginger, cinnamon, allspice, nutmeg, and cloves, and use a **whisk** to *whisk* together. Set the bowl aside. In a **small bowl**, whisk together the whole egg, egg yolk, molasses, and vanilla until combined. Set this bowl aside, too.

4. **Cream the butter and brown sugar together.** Place the butter and brown sugar in a **large mixing bowl**. Using a **handheld electric mixer** set to medium speed ⚠ , *cream* the mixture together for 5 minutes or until it's light and fluffy. Pour in

continues

the egg mixture and *beat* for 2 minutes. Stop the mixer, scrape down the sides of the bowl with a **rubber spatula,** and beat for 1 minute more.

5. **Combine the wet and dry ingredients.** Use the rubber spatula to *fold* the flour mixture into the butter-sugar mixture until the dough is fully mixed.

6. **Portion the cookies.** Scoop out about ¼ cup of dough, and use your hands to roll it into a ball. Squish the ball onto the plate with the crinkle coating to form a disk about ½ inch thick. Place the cookie on one of the prepared baking sheets with the crinkle coating side up. Repeat with the remaining dough, leaving 3 inches between the cookies. Transfer two of the baking sheets to the oven. ⚠

7. **Bake the cookies for 14 to 15 minutes.** The cookies are done when the sugar crust is crinkled and golden brown. Using **oven mitts,** remove the pans from the oven ⚠ , place on a **wire cooling rack,** and let the cookies cool on the pans for 20 minutes before eating.

8. **Bake more batches.** Repeat step 7 with the remaining dough.

Baker's Notes

What went well? How can you improve next time?

RECIPE: ....

NOTES: ....

....

....

....

....

....

....

....

....

....

....

....

Chocolate Chippers 2.0

Prep time:
50 minutes

Bake time:
12 minutes
per batch

Cool time:
15 minutes
per batch

Yield:
24 cookies

Ingredients

3½ cups all-purpose flour

1 teaspoon salt

½ teaspoon baking soda

3 large eggs

2 tablespoons heavy cream

1½ teaspoons vanilla extract

1¾ cups (3½ sticks) butter, **softened** *

½ cup granulated sugar

1¾ cups packed brown sugar

2 cups semisweet chocolate chips

*Turn to page 15 to learn
how to soften butter.

Instructions

1. **Preheat the oven to 350°F and prepare the baking sheets.** Before turning on the oven, adjust 2 oven racks to the middle-most positions in the oven—not too close to the top or bottom. Line **3 baking sheets** with **parchment paper**.

2. **Begin making the dough.** In a **medium mixing bowl**, *combine* the flour, salt, and baking soda and use a **whisk** to mix them together. In a **small bowl**, *whisk* together the eggs, cream, and vanilla. Set both bowls aside.

3. **Cream the butter and sugars together.** In a **large mixing bowl**, *combine* the butter, granulated sugar, and brown sugar. Using a **handheld electric mixer** set to medium speed ⚠ , *cream* the mixture for 5 minutes, until it's light and fluffy. Add half of the egg mixture and *beat* for 30 seconds. Then, add the remaining egg mixture and continue beating for 30 seconds. Stop the mixer, scrape down the sides of the bowl with a **rubber spatula**, and continue to beat for 2 minutes more.

4. **Combine the wet and dry ingredients.** With the rubber spatula, gently *fold* the flour mixture into the wet mixture until a dough forms. Measure out about 1½ cups of dough and, using a **small spoon**, scoop it into 8 even balls. Place them on 1 of the prepared baking sheets. These will be a special first batch, which you will crush into crumbs (more on this later). Press the balls down with the back of the spoon to form disks.

5. **Bake this special batch of cookies for 18 minutes.** Place the baking sheet in the oven ⚠ and bake for 18 minutes. They are done when they are crispy and dark brown. Using **oven mitts**, remove the cookies from the oven ⚠ and place them on a **wire cooling rack** to cool for 20 minutes. Leave the oven on.

continues

6. **Smash the cookies into crumbs.** Break the cookies*
    into chunks with your hands, and place them in a **large
    plastic bag.** Place the bag between **2 kitchen towels**
    on the counter. Using a **rolling pin**, gently pound
    and roll until the cookie pieces are finely crushed
    into crumbs.

7. **Fold the crumbs back into the dough.** Re-line the
    baking sheet with parchment paper. Using the rubber
    spatula, gently *fold* the cookie crumbs and chocolate
    chips into the remaining dough.

8. **Portion the dough.** Using the small spoon, scoop 8 or
    9 dough balls onto each prepared baking sheet, spac-
    ing them 3 inches apart. Press down with the back of
    the spoon to form disks, and place the baking sheets
    in the oven. ⚠

9. **Bake the cookies for 10 to 12 minutes.** You'll know
    they're done when the edges are golden brown. Using
    the oven mitts, remove the pans from the oven ⚠,
    place them on the wire cooling rack, and let the cook-
    ies cool on the pans for 15 minutes.

10. **Bake more batches:** Repeat step 9 with the remaining
    dough. Eat the cookies while they're warm, or dunk
    them in milk!

Baker's Notes

What went well? How can you improve next time?

RECIPE: ....

NOTES: ....

....

....

....

....

....

....

....

....

....

....

....

Cowgirl Squares

Prep time:
30 minutes

Bake time:
18 minutes

Cool time:
30 minutes

Yield:
15 squares

Ingredients

Nonstick cooking spray

3¾ cups all-purpose flour

1 teaspoon baking soda

1 teaspoon salt

½ teaspoon ground cinnamon

3 large eggs

¼ cup molasses

2 teaspoons vanilla extract

1½ cups (3 sticks) butter, softened*

2½ cups packed brown sugar

1 (11-ounce) bag butterscotch chips

2 cups sweetened shredded coconut

1½ cups chopped nuts of your choice

1 cup dried tart cherries

*Turn to page 15 to learn how to soften butter.

Instructions

1. **Preheat the oven to 350°F and prepare the baking sheet.** Coat a **baking sheet** evenly with nonstick cooking spray (don't forget to coat the sides!). Line the bottom of the pan with a piece of **parchment paper**, then spray the parchment, too.

2. **Prepare the dry and wet ingredients.** In a **medium mixing bowl**, *combine* the flour, baking soda, salt, and cinnamon and use a **whisk** to *whisk* together. Set the bowl aside. In a **small bowl**, whisk together the eggs, molasses, and vanilla until combined. Set the bowl aside.

3. **Cream the butter and brown sugar together.** Place the butter and brown sugar in a **large mixing bowl**. Using a **handheld electric mixer** set to medium speed ⚠ , *cream* the mixture together for 5 minutes or until it's light and fluffy. Pour in the egg mixture and *beat* for 2 minutes. Stop the mixer, scrape down the sides of the bowl with a **rubber spatula**, and beat for 1 minute more.

4. **Fold in the dry ingredients.** Using the rubber spatula, gently *fold* in the flour mixture until it is just combined. Then, fold in the butterscotch chips, coconut, nuts, and cherries until evenly mixed. Pour the dough onto the prepared baking sheet and use your hands to spread it out evenly. Place the baking sheet in the oven. ⚠

5. **Bake for 16 to 18 minutes.** The squares are done when the top is evenly golden brown and it passes the **Toothpick Test** (see page 16). Using **oven mitts**, remove the squares from the oven ⚠ and place them on a **wire cooling rack** to cool in the pan for 30 minutes.

6. **Cut and serve.** Set the baking sheet with a long side facing you. Using a **pizza wheel** ⚠ , make 4 cuts evenly spaced from the top to the bottom of the rectangle and 2 evenly spaced cuts the long way (from left to right). This will give you 15 squares. Serve warm.

Pineapple-Coconut Macaroonies

Prep time:
1 hour

Bake time:
25 minutes
per batch

Cool time:
20 minutes
per batch

Yield:
16 to 18 cookies

Ingredients

2 tablespoons butter

2 tablespoons packed brown sugar

1 (20-ounce) can crushed pineapple, with
its juice

1 teaspoon vanilla extract

Nonstick cooking spray

4 cups sweetened shredded coconut

4 large **egg whites** *

¼ teaspoon salt

2 tablespoons sugar

*Turn to page 14 to learn
how to separate eggs.

Instructions

1. **Caramelize*** **the pineapple.** Place a **large skillet** on the stovetop over medium-high heat. ⚠ Melt the butter in the pan until it starts to sizzle, then add the brown sugar and stir with a **heat-resistant spatula**. Add the pineapple and the juice from the can and stir again to evenly coat it in the sugar. Turn the heat down to low and cook slowly for 30 minutes (no need to stir). The pineapple is done when the edges are golden brown and the moisture has completely evaporated. Remove the skillet from the hot burner ⚠ and let cool for 15 minutes. Then, stir in the vanilla with the spatula.

   *When you caramelize an ingredient, you are heating it until all the water inside it evaporates, leaving just the sugar, which will start to cook. When you cook sugar, it turns into delightfully delicious caramel!

2. **Preheat the oven to 350°F and prepare the baking sheets.** Before turning on the oven, adjust 2 oven racks to the middle-most positions in the oven—not too close to the top or bottom. Line **2 baking sheets** with **parchment paper** and coat the parchment with nonstick cooking spray.

3. **Mix the fruit together.** Using **oven mitts** if the handle of the skillet is hot, use the heat-resistant spatula to scrape the pineapple into a **large mixing bowl**. Add the coconut and use the spatula to *toss* the pineapple and coconut together until well combined.

4. **Whip the egg whites.** Pour the egg whites into a **medium mixing bowl** and add the salt. Using a **handheld electric mixer** set to medium speed ⚠ , *whip* the egg whites for 1 minute. Stop the mixer and sprinkle in half of the sugar. Increase the

continues

*The Beak Peaks Test (see page 16) can help you figure out whether your egg whites are at the soft peaks stage.

speed to the highest setting, whip for 1 more minute, then stop it again. Add the rest of the sugar and continue whipping for 1 minute. You're done when the egg whites are super glossy and slightly firm, forming soft peaks.*

5. **Add the egg whites to the fruit.** Using a **rubber spatula**, gently *fold* the whipped egg whites into the fruit until it has just combined. Do not overmix or you'll knock the air out of the egg whites.

6. **Portion the macaroonies onto the baking sheets.** Use a **spoon** to place 8 or 9 small heaps on each baking sheet, spacing them 3 inches apart. Press down on each macaroon with the back of the spoon to gently flatten it a little. Place the baking sheets in the oven. ⚠

7. **Bake for 20 to 25 minutes.** They're done when the coconut tips are deep golden brown. Using the oven mitts, remove the pans from the oven ⚠ , place them on a **wire cooling rack**, and let the macaroonies cool on the pans for 20 minutes before serving.

8. **Bake the second batch.** Repeat steps 6 and 7 with any remaining batter while the first batch cools.

Baker's Notes

What went well? How can you improve next time?

RECIPE: ....

NOTES: ....

....

....

....

....

....

....

....

....

....

....

....

....

Chewy Fudge Brownies

Prep time:
30 minutes

Bake time:
45 minutes

Cool time:
1 hour

Yield:
15 brownies

Ingredients

Nonstick cooking spray

2 cups semisweet chocolate chips

1 cup store-bought caramel sauce

2 cups all-purpose flour

¼ cup unsweetened cocoa powder

1½ teaspoons salt

5 large eggs

1 tablespoon vanilla extract

1½ cups (3 sticks) butter, softened*

2½ cups granulated sugar

¾ cup packed brown sugar

*Turn to page 15 to learn how to soften butter.

Instructions

1. **Preheat the oven to 350°F and prepare the baking sheet.** Coat a **baking sheet** evenly with nonstick cooking spray (don't forget to coat the sides!). Line the bottom of the baking sheet with **parchment paper**, then spray the parchment, too.

2. **Melt the chocolate and caramel sauce.** In a **medium microwave-safe bowl**, *combine* the chocolate chips and caramel sauce. Microwave for 2 minutes to 2 minutes 30 seconds, stopping every 30 seconds to stir with a **spoon**, until it's completely melted. Set the hot bowl aside to cool while you continue the recipe. ⚠

3. **Prepare the dry and wet ingredients.** In a **medium mixing bowl**, *combine* the flour, cocoa powder, and salt and use a **whisk** to *whisk* together. Set the bowl aside. Crack the eggs one at a time into a **small bowl**, then add the vanilla and whisk until combined. Set the bowl aside.

4. **Cream the butter and sugars together.** Place the butter, granulated sugar, and brown sugar in a **large mixing bowl**. Using a **handheld electric mixer** set to medium speed ⚠ , *cream* the mixture together for 5 minutes or until it's light and fluffy. Add half of the egg mixture and *beat* for 30 seconds. Then, add the remaining egg mixture and continue beating for 30 seconds. Stop the mixer, scrape down the sides of the bowl with a **rubber spatula**, and continue to beat for 2 minutes more.

5. **Finish the batter.** Pour in the melted caramel and chocolate mixture and mix for 1 minute more. Set the mixer aside, and *fold* in the dry ingredients with the rubber spatula. Pour the batter onto the prepared baking sheet and spread evenly with the rubber spatula. Place the baking sheet in the oven. ⚠

continues

6. **Bake the brownies for 40 to 45 minutes.** They are done when the top is glossy and crackled. Using **oven mitts,** remove the brownies from the oven ⚠ and place them on a **wire cooling rack** to cool in the pan for 1 hour.

7. **Cut and serve.** Set the baking sheet with a long side facing you. Using a **pizza wheel** ⚠ , make 4 cuts evenly spaced from the top to the bottom of the rectangle and 2 evenly spaced cuts the long way (from left to right). This will give you 15 brownies. Serve warm.

Baker's Notes

What went well? How can you improve next time?

RECIPE: ....

NOTES: ....

....

....

....

....

....

....

....

....

....

....

....

Chocolate Raspberry Bars

Prep time:
45 minutes

Bake time:
30 minutes

Cool time:
30 minutes

Yield:
15 bars

Ingredients

For the crust

Nonstick cooking spray

4 cups all-purpose flour

¾ cup packed brown sugar

1 teaspoon salt

1½ cups (3 sticks) butter, **softened***

⅓ cup ice water

For the filling and topping

1¼ cups semisweet chocolate chips, *divided*

1 (14-ounce) can sweetened condensed milk

1 cup raspberry jam, *divided*

4 cups frozen raspberries, *divided*

*Turn to page 15 to learn how to soften butter.

Instructions

1. **Preheat the oven to 425°F and prepare the baking sheets.** Coat a **baking sheet** evenly with nonstick cooking spray (don't forget to coat the sides!). Line the bottom of the baking sheet with **parchment paper**, then spray the parchment, too.

2. **Make the crust.** In a **large mixing bowl**, *combine* the flour, brown sugar, and salt, and use a **whisk** to *whisk* everything together. Add the butter and, using a **large fork or pastry blender**, *cut in the butter* with the flour mixture for about 5 minutes, until it looks rough and *shaggy*. Sprinkle the ice water over the dough and continue to *blend* with the large fork or pastry blender for 2 minutes. Measure out 1½ cups of dough for your topping and set it aside. Place the rest of the dough on the prepared baking sheet. Using your hands, press out the dough evenly to cover the entire sheet, making sure to press it up the sides of the baking sheet and into the corners. Place the crust in the oven. ⚠

3. **Bake the crust for 10 to 12 minutes.** When it's done, it should be firm and light golden brown. Using **oven mitts**, remove the crust from the oven ⚠ and place it on a **wire cooling rack** to cool for 20 minutes while you make the filling. Lower the oven temperature to 350°F.

4. **Make the filling.** In a **large microwave-safe bowl**, *combine* 1 cup of chocolate chips, the sweetened condensed milk, and ½ cup of raspberry jam. Heat in the microwave for 2 minutes, stopping to stir with a **heat-resistant spatula** after 1 minute. Continue heating and stirring until it's completely melted. Add 2 cups of frozen raspberries and stir well to smash them into the chocolate mixture. Pour the filling onto the baked crust and spread it evenly with the heat-resistant spatula.

continues

5. **Add the topping.** Remember the dough you set aside? Use your fingers to crumble it evenly over the filling, then sprinkle the remaining 2 cups of raspberries on as well, pressing them down into the filling. Use a **spoon** to put the remaining ½ cup of jam in a **small plastic bag**, then seal the bag and snip off one corner with **scissors** (you've just made a piping bag!). Squeeze lines of jam across the top of the filling until it's used up. Sprinkle the remaining ¼ cup of chocolate chips over the mix, and place the pan in the oven. ⚠

6. **Bake for 30 minutes.** The bars are done when the edges are deep golden brown. Using oven mitts, remove the bars from the oven ⚠ and set them on the wire cooling rack to cool in the pan for 30 minutes.

7. **Cut and serve.** Set the baking sheet with a long side facing you. Using a **pizza wheel** ⚠ , make 4 cuts evenly spaced from the top to the bottom of the rectangle and 2 evenly spaced cuts the long way (from left to right). This will give you 15 bars. Serve warm.

Baker's Notes

What went well? How can you improve next time?

RECIPE: ....

NOTES: ....

....

....

....

....

....

....

....

....

....

....

....

....

S'mores Bars

Prep time:
40 minutes

Bake time:
40 minutes

Cool time:
30 minutes

Yield:
15 bars

Ingredients

For the crust

Nonstick cooking spray

1 cup (2 sticks) butter

1⅓ (14.5-ounce) boxes graham crackers (4 sleeves)

½ cup packed brown sugar

For the filling

4 cups semisweet chocolate chips

1¼ cups (2½ sticks) butter, softened*

2½ cups packed brown sugar

5 large eggs

2 teaspoons vanilla extract

*Turn to page 15 to learn how to soften butter.

2 cups all-purpose flour

¾ cup unsweetened cocoa powder

1½ teaspoons salt

1½ teaspoons baking soda

For the toppings

⅓ (14.5-ounce) box graham crackers
  (1 sleeve)

2 cups milk chocolate chips

3 cups mini marshmallows

Instructions

1. **Preheat the oven to 325°F and prepare the baking sheets.** Coat a **baking sheet** evenly with nonstick cooking spray (don't forget to coat the sides!). Line the bottom of the baking sheet with **parchment paper**, then spray the parchment, too.

2. **Make the graham cracker crust.** Place the butter in a **small microwave-safe bowl** and microwave for 2 minutes or until melted. Set up a **food processor fitted with the metal blade attachment.** ⚠ Crumble the crackers into the processor bowl and add the brown sugar. Attach the lid and pulse the machine on and off until the crackers are fine crumbs. *Drizzle* in the melted butter and *blend* for 30 seconds. Pour the mixture onto the prepared baking sheet, and use your hands to press it evenly into the bottom and 1 inch up the sides of the pan. Place the crust in the oven. ⚠

3. **Bake for 12 to 15 minutes.** Using **oven mitts**, remove the crust from the oven ⚠ and place the pan on a **wire cooling rack** to cool for 20 minutes while you make the filling. Leave the oven on.

continues

4. **Begin making the filling.** Place the semisweet chocolate chips in a **small microwave-safe bowl** and microwave for 3 minutes, stopping every 30 seconds to stir with a **spoon**, until melted. Set the bowl aside.

5. **Cream the butter and brown sugar together.** Place the butter and brown sugar in a **large mixing bowl**. Using a **handheld electric mixer** set to medium speed ⚠, *cream* the mixture together for 5 minutes or until it's light and fluffy. Add the eggs, one at a time, and *beat* for 20 seconds after each addition. Add the vanilla and mix until it's combined, then pour in the melted chocolate and beat for 1 minute more. Set the chocolate mixture aside.

6. **Add the dry ingredients.** In a **medium mixing bowl**, *combine* the flour, cocoa powder, salt, and baking soda and use a **whisk** to *whisk* together. Use a **rubber spatula** to *fold* the flour mixture into the chocolate mixture until they are just combined. Pour the filling onto the crust and spread it evenly with the rubber spatula.

7. **Add the toppings.** Break the graham crackers into small pieces and poke them down evenly into the filling. Scatter the milk chocolate chips and marshmallows across the top and gently press them down until they stick. Place the baking sheet in the oven. ⚠

8. **Bake for 35 to 40 minutes.** The s'mores bars are done when the marshmallows are toasted and golden. Using oven mitts, remove the bars from the oven ⚠ and place the pan on the wire cooling rack to cool for 30 minutes.

9. **Cut and serve.** Set the baking sheet with a long side facing you. Using a **pizza wheel** ⚠, make 4 cuts evenly spaced from the top to the bottom of the rectangle and 2 evenly spaced cuts the long way (from left to right). This will give you 15 bars. Serve warm.

Baker's Notes

What went well? How can you improve next time?

RECIPE: ....

NOTES: ....

....

....

....

....

....

....

....

....

....

....

....

....

CHAPTER 4

Cakes and Cupcakes

Stackable Almond Crêpe Cakes with Lemon Cream

Prep time:
50 minutes

Bake time:
About 10 minutes

Yield:
6 to 8 (*3-inch*)
layer cakes

Ingredients

For the cakes

1¾ cups whole milk

1 teaspoon vanilla extract

4½ tablespoons butter, *divided*

½ cup almond flour

½ cup all-purpose flour

¼ teaspoon salt

2 tablespoons sugar

2 large eggs

Nonstick cooking spray

1½ tablespoons vegetable oil

A crêpe (pronounced "krehp" or "krape") is a thin French pancake. Crêpes are normally made in a pan on the stovetop, but this recipe shows you how to make them in the oven.

Ingredients continued

For the lemon cream

⅓ cup freshly squeezed lemon juice (from 2 to 3 lemons)

½ cup sugar

⅛ teaspoon salt

4 large egg yolks *

3 tablespoons cold butter

1 cup heavy cream

Powdered sugar, for *dusting*

*Turn to page 14 to learn how to separate eggs.

Instructions

1. **Begin making the cake batter.** In a **small microwave-safe bowl**, *combine* the milk and vanilla and microwave for 1 minute. Set the bowl aside. In a **separate small microwave-safe bowl**, microwave 3 tablespoons of butter for 30 seconds or until melted. Set this bowl aside, too.

2. **Mix the flours, sugar, and eggs for the batter.** In a **medium mixing bowl**, *sift* together the almond flour, all-purpose flour, salt, and sugar with a **sifter**. Use your fist to make a crater in the middle of the flour mixture. Crack the eggs into the crater and use a **whisk** to break up the yolks. Slowly, working from the inside out, let a little flour cave into the mixture as you *whisk,* until all the flour is mixed in.

3. **Finish the batter.** Pour in half of the warm milk mixture and *whisk* vigorously for 1 minute. Then, pour in the melted butter and whisk for 30 seconds. Pour in

continues

the remaining warm milk and whisk for 30 seconds more. Your batter will be super runny with the consistency of cream. Cover with **plastic wrap**.

4. **Preheat the oven to 450°F and prepare the baking sheets.** Before turning on the oven, adjust 2 oven racks to the middle-most positions in the oven—not too close to the top or bottom. Coat **2 baking sheets** evenly with nonstick cooking spray. In the same bowl you used to melt the butter earlier, *combine* the vegetable oil and the remaining 1½ tablespoons of butter. Microwave for 30 seconds or until melted. Using a **pastry brush**, brush the baking sheets with the mixture (you will need to *grease* your pans twice for this recipe).

5. **Heat the baking sheets.** Place the baking sheets in the oven for 5 minutes ⚠. Then, using 2 **oven mitts**, carefully remove the hot sheets ⚠ and set them on the stovetop. Pour half of the batter onto one hot sheet and, holding the sheet with both hands, tilt it every which way to cover the entire surface with a very thin layer of batter, then set it on the stovetop. Repeat with the second baking sheet and remaining batter. Return both sheets to the oven ⚠.

6. **Bake the cakes.** Bake for 30 seconds, then open the oven ⚠ and, using the oven mitts, rotate the baking sheets from front to back. Bake for 5 minutes, then open the oven carefully ⚠ (steam will escape) and rotate the baking sheets again. Bake for 5 more minutes, until the cakes are light golden with some large bubbles. Remove the baking sheets from the oven ⚠ and place them on **wire cooling racks** to cool while you continue the recipe.

*Lemon cream is made with lemon "curd," a thick filling made primarily from citrus fruits. The main ingredients are egg yolks, sugar, fruit juice, zest, and butter.

7. **Begin making the** lemon cream.* In a **small saucepan**, *combine* the lemon juice, sugar, and salt and stir with a **spoon.** Set over medium heat and warm until the sugar is dissolved and the juice is hot but not *boiling.* ⚠

8. *Temper* **the egg yolks.** Using a **butter knife**, cut the cold butter into chunks and set them aside. In a **medium mixing bowl**, use the whisk to *whisk* the egg yolks. Use a **ladle** to slowly *drizzle* the hot lemon juice into the yolks, whisking constantly. Then, pour the mixture back into the saucepan and place it over medium-low heat, whisking constantly for 3 to 4 minutes, until the mixture thickens. Remove the saucepan from the hot burner ⚠ and add the butter chunks, one at a time, stirring with a **heat-resistant spatula** until each is melted before adding the next. Set the saucepan aside.

9. **Cut the cake into circles.** Using a **3-inch round cookie cutter**, cut out as many circles of cake as you can from the baking sheets. You should be able to get 30 to 40 circles.

10. **Whip the cream.** Pour the cream into a **medium mixing bowl**. Using a **handheld electric mixer** set to the highest speed ⚠ , *whip* the cream for 4 to 5 minutes or until it forms stiff peaks.* Using a **rubber spatula**, stir half of the whipped cream into the cooled lemon sauce. Then, gently *fold* in the remaining cream.

> *The Beak Peaks Test (see page 16) can help you figure out whether your cream is whipped enough.

11. **Assemble the cakes.** Place a circle of cake on a **serving plate** and top with a small *dollop* of lemon cream. Layer on another cake circle and a spoonful of cream. Repeat until each cake has 4 or 5 layers. *Dust* with powdered sugar and serve.

Black and White Layer Cake

Prep time:
30 minutes

Bake time:
35 minutes

Cool time:
1 hour 30 minutes

Yield:
1 *(8-inch)*
layer cake

Ingredients

For the chocolate cake

Nonstick cooking spray

½ cup (1 stick) butter

2 cups whole milk, *divided*

2 cups sugar

1¾ cups all-purpose flour

1 teaspoon baking soda

1 teaspoon baking powder

¾ cup unsweetened cocoa powder

1 teaspoon salt

2 large eggs

1 large egg yolk*

2 teaspoons vanilla extract

*Turn to page 14 to learn how to separate eggs.

For the vanilla frosting

½ cup heavy cream

½ cup white chocolate chips

½ teaspoons salt

1 tablespoon vanilla extract

2½ cups (3 sticks) butter, softened*

2 cups powdered sugar

*Turn to page 15 to learn how to soften butter.

Instructions

1. **Preheat the oven to 350°F and prepare the pans.** Coat **2 (8-inch) cake pans** with nonstick cooking spray. Line the bottoms with circles* of **parchment paper,** then spray the parchment, too.

2. **Begin making the cake batter.** Place the butter in a **small microwave-safe bowl** and microwave for 30 seconds or until melted. Set the bowl aside. Pour 1 cup of milk into a **microwave-safe measuring cup** and microwave for 1½ to 2 minutes or until *boiling*. Set the hot measuring cup aside, too. ⚠

3. **Finish making the cake batter.** In a **large mixing bowl**, use a **whisk** to *whisk* together the sugar, flour, baking soda, baking powder, cocoa powder, and salt. Add the melted butter, whole eggs, egg yolk, remaining 1 cup of milk (that you didn't heat), and vanilla. Using a **handheld electric mixer** set to

*To make parchment circles that fit your pan perfectly, place the cake pan right-side up on top of the parchment, trace around the pan with a pencil, and then cut the circle ¼ inch smaller than the circle you drew.

continues

medium speed ⚠ , *beat* the ingredients together for 2 minutes. Pour in the hot milk and continue beating for 1 minute (the batter will be very thin). Pour the batter equally into the 2 prepared cake pans. Place them in the oven. ⚠

4. **Bake for 30 to 35 minutes.** The cakes are done when they pass the **Toothpick Test** (see page 16). Using **oven mitts**, remove the cakes from the oven ⚠ and set the pans on **wire cooling racks** to cool for 30 minutes. After that time, run a **butter knife** around the inside edges of the pans and turn them over to release the cakes from the pans. Peel the parchment circles off the bottoms and turn the cakes right-side up again on the wire cooling racks to cool for 30 minutes more. Place the cakes in the freezer for 30 minutes while you make the frosting.

5. **Melt the white chocolate for the frosting.** In a **small microwave-safe bowl**, stir together the heavy cream, white chocolate, salt, and vanilla with a **spoon**. Microwave for 1½ minutes, then remove and stir until completely melted.

6. **Finish the frosting.** In a **large mixing bowl**, use the handheld electric mixer set to medium speed ⚠ to *beat* the butter for 1 minute. Add the powdered sugar, reduce the speed to low, and mix for 30 seconds. Increase the speed to medium again and mix for 3 minutes. Pour in the melted chocolate mixture and mix the frosting for 1 minute more, until it's super creamy.

*The reason you flip the cakes upside down to stack and frost them is because the bottoms of the cakes are much flatter than the tops, which might dip in or dome out. Flipping the cake upside down makes the frosted cake look straighter (this is what professional bakers do!).

7. **Frost the cakes.** Flip one cake layer upside down onto a **serving platter**. Spoon 1 cup of frosting on top and spread it out evenly to the edges with the butter knife. Place the second layer **upside down*** on top of the first layer. Spoon the remaining frosting on top and spread it to cover the top and the sides. Cut into slices with a **sharp knife** ⚠ and serve!

Baker's Notes

What went well? How can you improve next time?

RECIPE: ....

NOTES: ....

....

....

....

....

....

....

....

....

....

....

....

Classic Yellow Cupcakes
with Butterscotch Frosting

Prep time:
45 minutes

Bake time:
18 minutes

Cool time:
55 minutes

Yield:
24 cupcakes

Ingredients

*Turn to page 15 to learn how to soften butter.

For the cupcakes

Nonstick cooking spray

¼ cup sour cream

½ cup whole milk

1 tablespoon vanilla extract

2¼ cups all-purpose flour

1½ teaspoons baking powder

¼ teaspoon baking soda

1 teaspoon salt

1 cup (2 sticks) butter, **softened***

1 cup sugar

⅔ cup packed brown sugar

3 large eggs

3 large egg yolks*

*Turn to page 14 to learn how to separate eggs.

For the frosting

¾ cup sour cream

1 cup butterscotch chips

½ teaspoon salt

1 tablespoon vanilla extract

1½ cups (3 sticks) butter, softened

2 cups powdered sugar

Instructions

1. **Preheat the oven to 350°F and prepare the pans.** Coat **2 muffin pans** with nonstick cooking spray, including the insides of the cups and the top of the pans. Place a **cupcake liner** inside each cup.

2. **Begin making the cupcake batter.** In a **small microwave-safe bowl**, *combine* the sour cream, milk, and vanilla. Microwave for 1 minute, then remove the bowl and stir with a **spoon**. In a **medium mixing bowl**, use a **sifter** to *sift* together the flour, baking powder, baking soda, and salt. Set both bowls aside.

3. **Cream the butter and sugar together.** Place the butter in a **large mixing bowl.** Using a **handheld electric mixer** set to medium speed ⚠ , *beat* the butter for 1 minute, then add both types of sugar. Beat for 30 seconds to *combine*. Increase the mixer speed to high and *cream* the mixture for 5 minutes or until it is very light and fluffy. Stop the mixer and scrape down the sides of the bowl with a **rubber spatula**.

4. **Add the eggs and milk.** Add the whole eggs and egg yolks to the batter 2 at a time and, using the mixer, *beat* for 20 seconds after each addition. Scrape down the sides of the bowl, then pour in the sour cream mixture and beat for 20 more seconds. Scrape down the bowl one more time.

continues

5. **Add the dry ingredients.** Use the rubber spatula to gently *fold* half of the flour mixture into the batter until fully mixed. Then, fold in the remaining flour mixture until just combined. Using an **ice cream scoop or large spoon**, fill each cupcake three-quarters full. Place the pans in the oven. ⚠

6. **Bake for 15 to 18 minutes.** The cupcakes are done when the tops are golden brown and they pass the **Toothpick Test** (see page 16). Using **oven mitts**, remove the pans from the oven ⚠ and set them on **wire cooling racks** to cool for 25 minutes. Then, remove the cupcakes from the pans and return them to the wire cooling racks to cool for 30 more minutes before frosting.

7. **Meanwhile, begin making the frosting.** In a **small microwave-safe bowl**, stir together the sour cream, butterscotch chips, salt, and vanilla with a **spoon**. Microwave for 1½ minutes, then remove the bowl and stir to melt the butterscotch entirely.

8. **Finish the frosting.** Place the butter in a **large mixing bowl**. Using the handheld electric mixer set to medium speed ⚠ , *beat* the butter for 1 minute. Add the powdered sugar, decrease the mixer speed to low, and *blend* together for 30 seconds. Increase the speed to medium again and beat for 3 minutes. Stop the mixer and pour in the butterscotch mixture. Beat the frosting for 1 minute more, until it's super creamy.

9. **Frost the cupcakes.** Using a **butter knife**, *generously* frost each cooled cupcake and serve!

Baker's Notes

What went well? How can you improve next time?

RECIPE: ....

NOTES: ....

....

....

....

....

....

....

....

....

....

....

Peanut Butter and Jelly Cheesecake

Prep time:
1 hour

Bake time:
1 hour 27 minutes

Cool time:
7 hours

Yield:
1 *(9-inch)*
cheesecake
(10 to 12 servings)

Ingredients

For the crust

Nonstick cooking spray

3 tablespoons butter

2 tablespoons creamy
   peanut butter

9 whole graham crackers (⅓ package)

1 cup dry-roasted peanuts

1 tablespoon sugar

For the cheesecake

4 cups (16 ounces) cream cheese

¾ cup creamy peanut butter

1¼ cups sugar

½ teaspoon salt

1 tablespoon vanilla extract

7 large eggs, *divided*

Ingredients continued

2 large egg yolks*

¾ cup grape jelly (or your favorite flavor)

*Turn to page 14 to learn how to separate eggs.

For the jelly topping

½ cup grape jelly (or your favorite flavor)

1 cup mixed fresh berries

⅛ teaspoon salt

1 teaspoon fresh lemon juice

Instructions

1. **Preheat the oven to 350°F and prepare the pan.** Coat a **9-inch springform pan** with nonstick cooking spray. Set it aside.

2. **Make the crust.** In a **small microwave-safe bowl**, *combine* the butter and peanut butter. Microwave for 45 seconds, until melted. Crumble the graham crackers into the bowl of a **food processor fitted with the metal blade attachment** ⚠, then add the peanuts and sugar. Cover and pulse the machine on and off until the crackers are fine crumbs. *Drizzle* in the melted peanut butter mixture and *blend* for 30 seconds or until fully combined. Transfer the mixture to the springform pan. Using your fingers, press the crust evenly over the bottom and three-quarters of the way (about 2 inches) up the sides of the pan. Place the pan in the oven. ⚠

3. **Bake the crust for 12 minutes.** Using **oven mitts**, remove the crust from the oven ⚠ and place it on a **wire cooling rack** to cool while you continue the recipe. Raise the oven temperature to 450°F.

continues

4. **Meanwhile, begin making the cheesecake batter.** Using a **butter knife**, cut the cream cheese into chunks, then transfer them to a **large microwave-safe bowl**. Add the peanut butter. Heat in the microwave for 1 minute, then remove the bowl and stir with a **rubber spatula**. Heat for 30 seconds more, then stir again.

5. **Combine the cream cheese and dry ingredients.** Using a **handheld electric mixer** set to medium speed ⚠ , *beat* the cream cheese mixture for 1 minute. Add the sugar, salt, and vanilla and beat for another 30 seconds, until combined. Increase the mixer speed to high and continue beating the mixture for 5 minutes. Stop the mixer and scrape down the sides of the bowl with the rubber spatula.

6. **Add the eggs and yolks.** Add 6 of the whole eggs and both of the egg yolks to the batter, 2 at a time, and *beat* with the mixer for 20 seconds after each addition. Scrape down the bowl again with the rubber spatula. Using a **large measuring cup**, measure out 1½ cups of batter and use a **whisk** to *whisk* the jelly into it. Set this "jelly batter" aside. Then, add the remaining whole egg to the large mixing bowl of batter, and use the handheld electric mixer to mix for 20 seconds. Gently pour the large bowl of batter into the cooled crust, scraping it out with the rubber spatula.

7. **Create a "jelly batter" swirl in the peanut butter batter.** Gently pour the reserved jelly batter in circles into the cheesecake. Using the butter knife, swirl the jelly batter around in 3 or 4 places, being careful to avoid the crust and not mix too much—you want to see the swirls.

8. **Prepare a water bath.** Fill a **pitcher** with 6 to 8 cups of very hot water from the sink. Wrap the outside of the springform pan with **aluminum foil** and place it in a **large roasting pan**. Using the oven mitts, pull the middle oven rack out a little bit and place the roasting pan with the cheesecake on it. ⚠ Gently pour the hot water from the pitcher into the roasting pan to create a *water bath*, being careful not to splash water into the cheesecake itself.

9. **Bake the cheesecake for 12 minutes.** Then, lower the oven temperature to 250°F. Continue baking for 1 hour 15 minutes. The cheesecake is done when it's a little browned, is jiggly, and has slightly cracked around the jelly swirls. Using the oven mitts, pull the oven rack out a little and carefully lift the cake from the water. ⚠ Be careful not to get the oven mitts wet. Gently set the pan on the wire cooling rack to cool for 3 hours. Then, cover the cheesecake tightly with **plastic wrap** and transfer it to the refrigerator to chill for 4 hours (or overnight).

10. **Make the jelly topping and serve.** In a **small bowl**, *combine* all the topping ingredients and mash them together with a **fork**.

11. **Serve.** Remove the cheesecake from the refrigerator and gently run a butter knife around the edges of the crust. Release the clamp on the side of the pan and remove the ring. Transfer the cheesecake (still on the metal base) to a large flat serving platter. * Cut into slices with a **sharp knife** ⚠ , and serve with a spoon-ful of jelly topping over each slice.

*It's possible to take the cheesecake off the metal base with a large metal spatula, but it can be challenging, so it's safer to leave it on the base. Just take care when cutting the cake into slices that you don't cut into the metal base.

Strawberry Pinwheel Cake

Prep time:
2 hours

Bake time:
14 minutes

Cool time:
15 minutes

Yield:
1 (18-inch)
roll cake
(8 to 10 servings)

TEST YOUR SKIllS

Ingredients

For the cake

Nonstick cooking spray

1½ cups all-purpose flour

½ teaspoon baking powder

1 tablespoon honey

½ teaspoon vanilla extract

2 tablespoons whole milk

4 large eggs

2 large **egg yolks***

¾ cup sugar

½ teaspoon salt

Powdered sugar, for *dusting*

> *Turn to page 14 to learn
> how to separate eggs.

Ingredients continued

For the filling

2 cups strawberries

1 cup strawberry jelly

2 tablespoons butter

½ cup heavy cream

For the frosting

½ cup (4 ounces) cream cheese, softened

½ cup (1 stick) butter, softened*

1 cup powdered sugar

½ cup strawberry jelly

1 teaspoon vanilla extract

⅛ teaspoon salt

Fresh strawberries, for *garnish*

*Turn to page 15 to learn how to soften butter. Use the same technique to soften the cream cheese in this recipe, too!

Instructions

1. **Preheat the oven to 350°F and prepare the pan.** Coat a **baking sheet** with non-stick cooking spray. Line the bottom of the baking sheet with **parchment paper**, then spray the parchment, too.

2. **Begin making the cake batter.** In a **medium mixing bowl**, use a **sifter** to *sift* the flour and baking powder together. In a **small bowl**, stir together the honey, vanilla, and milk with a **spoon**. Set both bowls aside.

continues

3. **Whip the eggs and sugar together.** In a **large mixing bowl**, *combine* the whole eggs and egg yolks. Using a **handheld electric mixer** set to medium speed ⚠ , *whip* the eggs and yolks together for 30 seconds, then add the sugar and salt. Increase the mixer speed to high and whip for 5 minutes. The mixture will be thick. Pour in the honey mixture and whip for 30 seconds more.

4. **Add the dry ingredients.** Sprinkle the flour mixture over the egg mixture. Gently *fold* with a **rubber spatula** until the flour is just mixed in, being careful not to overmix. Pour the batter onto the prepared baking sheet and spread it evenly with the rubber spatula. Place the pan in the oven. ⚠

5. **Bake the cake for 12 to 14 minutes.** It's done when it's light golden brown and passes the **Toothpick Test** (see page 16). Using **oven mitts**, remove the cake from the oven ⚠ and set the pan on a **wire cooling rack** to cool for 15 minutes while you continue the recipe.

6. **Make the filling.** Using a **sharp knife** ⚠ , cut the stems off the strawberries and discard them, then chop the berries into small pieces. In a **medium microwave-safe bowl**, *combine* the jelly and butter. Microwave for 1 minute, then remove it from the microwave and stir with a **fork** to combine. Add the cut strawberries and use the fork to smash them into the mixture. Stir in the cream.

7. **Roll the cake.** Clear off a clean surface and lay out a large piece of parchment paper. *Dust* the parchment with powdered sugar. Run a **butter knife** around the edges of the cake to release it from the baking sheet, and flip it out onto the sugar-dusted parchment. Peel off the parchment from the bottom of the cake and discard it. Pick up one long edge of the parchment the cake is currently sitting on, and use your hands to roll up the cake into a spiral (there will be parchment inside the spiral of the cake). Turn the cake roll so the seam is on the bottom, and let the cake rest for 15 minutes.

8. **Fill the cake.** Gently unroll the cake and use the rubber spatula to spread the filling over the inside, pressing a little so it soaks into the cake. Starting at the long edge, reroll the cake into a spiral (no parchment should go inside this time). Try to keep the spiral as tight as possible. When completely rolled, wrap the cake with parchment again and twist the ends of the paper like a Tootsie Roll. Lay the cake on a **baking sheet** and place it in the freezer for 1 hour.

9. **Make the frosting.** In a **medium mixing bowl**, *combine* the cream cheese and butter. Using the handheld electric mixer set to low speed ⚠ , *blend* them together for 1 minute. Add the powdered sugar and blend until combined. Increase the mixer speed to high and *whip* for 3 minutes, until the frosting is light and fluffy. Add the jelly, vanilla, and salt and continue whipping for 1 minute more, until fully blended.

10. **Frost the cake.** Remove the cake from the freezer and unwrap the parchment. Set the cake on a **serving platter**. Using the butter knife, spread the frosting all over the cake.

11. **Serve.** Use the sharp knife ⚠ to cut the cake into slices. *Garnish* with fresh strawberries.

Flourless Chocolate Cake

Prep time:
30 minutes

Bake time:
1 hour

Cool time:
5 hours

Yield:
1 *(8-inch)* cake
(6 to 8 servings)

TEST YOUR SKIllS

Ingredients

Nonstick cooking spray

¾ cup granulated sugar, *divided*

6 cold large eggs

1 tablespoon vanilla extract

10 ounces dark chocolate (from a bar, not chocolate chips)

10 tablespoons butter

¼ teaspoon salt

Powdered sugar or whipped cream and fresh fruit, for *garnish* (optional)

Instructions

1. **Preheat the oven to 300°F and prepare the cake pan.** Before turning the oven on, adjust an oven rack to the middle position. Coat an **8-inch cake pan** with nonstick cooking spray and line the bottom with a circle* of **parchment paper**. Spray the top of the parchment paper with more nonstick cooking spray after you put it in the pan.

2. **Set up the bowls of sugar.** Put 6 tablespoons of granulated sugar in a **small bowl** (this will be added to the egg whites). Put the remaining 6 tablespoons of granulated sugar in **another small bowl** (this will be mixed with the egg yolks). Set both of them aside for later.

3. **Separate the eggs.** Crack the eggs into a **large mixing bowl**. Then, with your hand, carefully scoop up 1 yolk at a time and gently wiggle your fingers to let the egg white drip through, being very careful not to **break the yolk**.* As you do this, transfer the yolk to a **small bowl** and add the vanilla. Set both of these bowls aside.

*To make a parchment circle that fits your pan perfectly, place the cake pan right-side up on top of the parchment, trace around the pan with a pencil, then cut the circle ¼ inch smaller than the circle you drew.

*Egg whites will not whip up properly with any speck of yolk residue in them.

continues

4. **Combine the chocolate and butter.** Using a **sharp knife** ⚠ , cut the chocolate and butter into chunks. Transfer them to a **medium microwave-safe bowl** and add the salt. Microwave for 30 seconds, then stop and stir thoroughly with a **spoon**. Do this 3 more times, until the chocolate is completely melted. Let the mixture cool for a few minutes while you continue the recipe—the mixture should be warm, not hot.

*The Beak Peaks Test (see page 16) can help you figure out whether your egg whites are whipped enough.

5. **Whip the egg whites.** Place a **damp kitchen towel** under the bowl with the egg whites so it doesn't move around when you *whip* the eggs. Have the bowl of sugar you set aside for the egg whites nearby. Using a **handheld electric mixer** set to medium speed ⚠ , begin to whip the egg whites. When large bubbles form, sprinkle in about 2 tablespoons of the sugar you set aside for the egg whites. Increase the mixer speed to high and continue to whip for 30 seconds. Add another 2 tablespoons of the sugar and whip on high for 1 minute. Add the remaining sugar for the egg whites and continue whipping for 3 to 4 more minutes, until the egg whites are firm, glossy, and holding stiff peaks.*

6. **Add the egg yolks to the chocolate.** Take the sugar you set aside for the egg yolks and pour it into the bowl with the egg yolks and vanilla. *Whisk* it lightly with a **whisk**, then pour this mixture into the warm chocolate mixture and whisk together thoroughly.

7. **Mix the whipped whites into the chocolate.** Take about one-third of the whipped egg whites and *sacrifice* them thoroughly into the chocolate mixture with the whisk. Then, pour the chocolate mixture into the bowl with the remaining whipped egg whites and gently *fold* them together with a **rubber spatula**

(do not use a whisk for this part, or the air you whipped into the egg whites might deflate!). Do not overmix—it's okay for some streaks of egg white to show. Gently pour the batter into the prepared cake pan.

8. **Prepare a water bath.** Fill a **pitcher** with 6 to 8 cups of very hot water from the sink. Place the full cake pan in a **large roasting pan**. Using **oven mitts** ⚠ , pull the middle oven rack slightly out and place the roasting pan on it. Slowly pour the hot water from the pitcher into the roasting pan around the cake to create a *water bath*, being careful not to splash water into the cake itself.

9. **Bake the cake for 1 hour.** You'll know it's done when the cake has slightly pulled away from the sides of the pan and is still a little jiggly in the center. Using the oven mitts, pull the oven rack out a little and carefully lift the cake out of the *water bath.* ⚠ Be careful not to get the oven mitts wet. Gently set the cake on a **wire cooling rack** for 45 minutes to 1 hour to cool completely. Then, move the cake to the refrigerator to chill for at least 4 hours (or overnight).

10. **Remove the cake from the pan.** Run a **butter knife** around the edges of the cake. Have your **serving platter** ready. Place a piece of parchment paper over the top of the cake, and then invert a **large plate** over the parchment. Hold everything together and flip it over—the cake will release from the pan upside down onto the plate. Remove the parchment circle from the bottom of the cake. Place your serving platter over the bottom of the cake, then flip your cake again so it's right-side up. Remove the parchment from the top.

11. **Cut into slices and serve!** If you want, you can *dust* the whole cake with powdered sugar, or serve individual slices with a *dollop* of whipped cream and fresh fruit.

Pies and Tarts

Tart Cherry Pouches

Prep time:
1 hour 30 minutes

Bake time:
40 minutes

Cool time:
15 minutes

Yield: 8 small pies

Ingredients

For the dough

½ lemon

2½ cups all-purpose flour,
  plus more for rolling the dough

2 tablespoons packed brown sugar

1 teaspoon salt

½ teaspoon ground cinnamon

1 cup (2 sticks) cold butter

1 large **egg yolk**✱

⅓ cup ice water

Nonstick cooking spray

✱Turn to page 14 to learn
how to separate eggs.

Ingredients continued

For the filling

1 lemon

1 (21-ounce) can tart cherry pie filling

2 tablespoons instant tapioca

1 teaspoon vanilla extract

⅛ teaspoon salt

2 tablespoons cold butter

For the egg wash

1 large egg

1 tablespoon whole milk

⅛ teaspoon salt

Sugar, for sprinkling

Instructions

1. **Begin making the dough.** Using the smallest holes on a **box grater** (or a **Microplane zester** if you have one), *zest* the half lemon into a **large mixing bowl**. ⚠ Add the flour, brown sugar, salt, and cinnamon and *whisk* together with a **fork**. Using a **butter knife**, cut the butter into small cubes and sprinkle them into the flour mixture. Using a **pastry blender or large fork**, *cut in the butter* with the flour mixture for about 5 minutes or until it looks rough and *shaggy*.

2. **Add the wet ingredients to the dough.** In a **small bowl**, *whisk* together the egg yolk and ice water with the fork and *drizzle* it over the dough. Using the pastry blender or large fork, roughly mix for 30 seconds. Then, rub the mixture between your fingers for 1 minute or until it's mostly combined but still crumbly. Divide the dough into 8 even pieces. Shape them into balls, squash them down to form disks, and place them on a **large plate**. Wrap the plate tightly with **plastic wrap** and refrigerate for 1 hour.

3. **Meanwhile, make the filling.** Using the box grater or Microplane, *zest* the lemon into a **medium mixing bowl**. Use a **sharp knife** ⚠ to slice the zested

continues

lemon in half, and squeeze 1 tablespoon lemon juice into the bowl with the zest (remove any seeds). Add the cherry pie filling, instant tapioca, vanilla, and salt and stir with a **large spoon**. Using the butter knife, cut the butter into 8 cubes. Set the bowl of filling and the butter aside.

4. **Preheat the oven to 350°F and prepare the baking sheets.** Before turning on the oven, adjust 2 oven racks to the middle-most positions in the oven—not too close to the top or bottom. Line **2 baking sheets** with **parchment paper**. Coat the parchment with nonstick cooking spray.

5. **Roll out the dough.** Clear off a clean surface and *dust* it lightly with flour. Working one at a time, place a dough disk on the floured counter. Sprinkle a little more flour on top of the disk and rub some onto a **rolling pin**. Roll each disk into a circle that measures 6 inches across.

6. **Fill the pouches.** Place ¼ cup of filling into the middle of each circle. Place one of the butter pieces in the center of the filling. Fold the crust over to form a half-moon shape, and *crimp* the edges with the fork to seal in the filling. Transfer the pouches to one of the prepared baking sheets, placing 4 pies on each baking sheet.

7. **Brush the pouches with an egg wash.** In a **small bowl**, *whisk* together the egg, milk, and salt with the fork. Using a **pastry brush**, brush a thin layer of egg wash over each pouch, and sprinkle some sugar on top. Using the sharp knife ⚠, cut 3 small slits in the tops of the pies to create steam vents. Place the baking sheets in the oven. ⚠

8. **Bake the pouches for 20 minutes.** Then, using **oven mitts**, open the oven and rotate the baking sheets from front to back. ⚠ Continue baking for another 20 minutes. The pouches are done when they're golden brown (it's okay if a little filling has bubbled out). Using oven mitts, remove the pouches from the oven ⚠ and set the pans on **wire cooling racks** to cool for 15 minutes before serving.

Baker's Notes

What went well? How can you improve next time?

RECIPE: ....

NOTES: ....

....

....

....

....

....

....

....

....

....

....

....

Huckleberry Blues Pie

Prep time:
1 hour 40 minutes

Bake time:
50 minutes

Cool time:
4 hours

Yield:
1 *(9-inch)* pie
(8 to 10 servings)

Ingredients

For the pie dough

1 lemon

2½ cups all-purpose flour,
plus more for rolling the dough

2 tablespoons packed brown sugar

1 teaspoon salt

1 cup (2 sticks) very cold butter,
plus 1 tablespoon softened*

1 large egg yolk*

⅓ cup ice water

> *Turn to page 15 to learn
> how to soften butter.

> *Turn to page 14 to learn
> how to separate eggs.

For the filling

Reserved lemon from making the pie dough

8 cups frozen huckleberries*

¾ cup packed brown sugar

2 tablespoons instant tapioca

¼ teaspoon salt

3 tablespoons cold butter

For the egg wash

1 large egg

1 tablespoon whole milk

⅛ teaspoon salt

Sugar, for sprinkling

*Huckleberries are wild blueberries. If you can't find them at the store, use regular frozen blueberries instead.

Instructions

1. **Begin making the pie dough.** Using the smallest holes on a **box grater** (or a **Microplane zester** if you have one), *zest* half the lemon (keeping the lemon whole) into a **large mixing bowl.** ⚠ Set the half-zested lemon aside for the filling. Add the flour, brown sugar, and salt and *whisk* with a **fork**. Using a **butter knife**, cut the 1 cup of cold butter into small cubes and sprinkle them into the flour mixture. Using a **pastry blender or large fork**, *cut in the butter* with the flour mixture for about 5 minutes, until it looks rough and *shaggy*.

continues

2. **Add the wet ingredients to the dough.** In a **small bowl**, *whisk* together the egg yolk and ice water with the fork. *Drizzle* it over the dough. Using the pastry blender or large fork, roughly mix for 30 seconds. Then, rub the mixture between your fingers for 1 minute, until it's mostly combined but still crumbly. Divide the dough in half, shape the halves into balls, and squash them down to form disks. Wrap each disk tightly with **plastic wrap** and refrigerate for 1 hour. Wash the large mixing bowl to use again.

3. **Meanwhile, make the filling.** Using the box grater or Microplane, *zest* the rest of the lemon into the large mixing bowl. Then, use a **sharp knife** ⚠ to slice the zested lemon in half, and squeeze 1 tablespoon lemon juice into the bowl with the zest (remove any seeds). Add the huckleberries, brown sugar, instant tapioca, and salt and stir with a **large spoon**. Smash some of the berries against the side of the bowl to create more juice. Let the filling sit at room temperature for 30 minutes to 1 hour. (It should be ready at the same time your dough is done chilling.) Using the butter knife, cut the butter into small pieces and set them aside.

4. **Preheat the oven to 425°F and prepare the pie plate.** Using your fingers, thoroughly *grease* a **9-inch glass pie plate** with the remaining 1 tablespoon of softened butter.

5. **Roll out the bottom crust.** Clear off a clean surface and *dust* it lightly with flour. Place one of the dough disks on the floured counter. Sprinkle a little more flour on top of the disk and rub some onto a **rolling pin**. Roll out the disk to form a circle that measures 12 inches across. Carefully wrap the dough around the rolling pin, then unroll the dough into the prepared pie plate. Using your hands, gently press the dough down into the dish, smoothing to remove any trapped air bubbles. Use a pair of clean **scissors** to trim the edges of the dough all the way around, leaving 1 inch of dough to hang over all sides of the dish.

6. **Fill the pie and add the top crust.** Pour the filling into the bottom crust and scatter the butter pieces over the top of the filling. Using the same technique as the bottom crust, roll out the remaining dough disk to form the top crust. Pick it up and center it over the filling. Using your hands, gently smooth the crust over the filling. Trim off the excess dough around the edges with the butter knife, keeping a 1-inch border like before. Fold the overlapping top crust under the bottom, then tuck it into the sides of the pie plate to form a thick lip. *Crimp* the dough evenly around the edges with the fork to seal in the filling.

7. **Brush with an egg wash.** In a **small bowl**, *whisk* together the egg, milk, and salt with the fork. Using a **pastry brush**, brush a thin layer of egg wash over the pie, and sprinkle some sugar on top. Using the sharp knife ⚠ , cut 5 small slits in a starburst pattern in the center of the pie to create steam vents. Place the pie on a **baking sheet** and place in the oven. ⚠

8. **Bake the pie for 15 minutes.** Then, lower the oven temperature to 350°F and continue baking for 30 to 35 minutes more. The pie is done when the crust is golden brown and the filling is bubbling and oozing out. Using **oven mitts**, remove the pie from the oven ⚠ and set it on a **wire cooling rack**. Let the pie rest for 4 hours or until it's completely cool before cutting and serving.

Give this pie a sweet and tangy kick by serving each slice topped with a *dollop* of sweetened sour cream! In a small bowl, whisk together 1½ cups sour cream with 5 tablespoons powdered sugar.

Puckerlicious Lemon Tart

Prep time:
45 minutes

Bake time:
45 minutes

Cool time:
3 hours

Yield: 1 (9-inch) tart (8 to 10 servings)

Ingredients

For the tart dough

7 tablespoons cold butter, plus
1 tablespoon **softened butter***

1 lemon

1 cup all-purpose flour

¼ teaspoon salt

3 tablespoons brown sugar

1 large egg yolk*

1 tablespoon ice water

Nonstick cooking spray

> *Turn to page 15 to learn how to soften butter.

> *Turn to page 14 to learn how to separate eggs.

Ingredients continued

For the filling

2 lemons

¾ cup granulated sugar

½ teaspoon salt

Reserved lemon from making the tart dough

½ cup (1 stick) butter, softened

2 tablespoons cornstarch

1 large egg

2 egg yolks

Instructions

1. **Preheat the oven to 375°F and prepare the tart pan.** Using your fingers, thoroughly *grease* a **9-inch tart pan** with the 1 tablespoon of softened butter.

2. **Begin making the tart dough.** Using the smallest holes on a **box grater** (or a **Microplane zester** if you have one), *zest* the entire lemon into a **large mixing bowl.** ⚠ (Set the whole zested lemon aside to use in the filling.) Add the flour, salt, and brown sugar and *whisk* with a **fork**. Using a **butter knife,** cut the 7 tablespoons cold butter into small cubes, and sprinkle them into the flour mixture. Using a **pastry blender or large fork,** *cut in the butter* with the flour mixture for about 5 minutes or until it looks rough and *shaggy*.

3. **Add the wet ingredients to the dough.** In a **small bowl,** *whisk* together the egg yolk and ice water with the fork. *Drizzle* it over the dough. Using the pastry blender or large fork, roughly mix for 30 seconds. Then, rub the mixture between your fingers for 1 minute or until it's mostly combined but still crumbly.

4. **Press the dough into the tart pan.** Transfer the dough to the prepared tart pan. Using your fingers, firmly press out the dough to evenly cover the bottom and up the sides of the pan. Use the fork to prick the dough 20 to 30 times all over.

continues

5. *Blind bake* the tart shell. Using **scissors**, cut out a circle of **parchment paper** that measures 12 inches across. Coat it lightly with nonstick cooking spray and place it over the tart dough, spray-side down. Pour 1½ cups uncooked rice or beans* on top of the parchment to weight down the dough. Place the tart pan on a **baking sheet** and transfer to the oven. ⚠ Bake for 20 minutes. Using **oven mitts**, remove the baking sheet with the tart shell from the oven ⚠ and place it on a **wire cooling rack**. Carefully remove the parchment and rice or beans, and let the tart cool on the baking sheet for 15 minutes while you continue the recipe. Leave the oven on, but reduce the temperature to 300°F.

6. **Meanwhile, begin making the filling.** Scrub the 2 lemons under cold water to clean them, then use a **sharp knife** ⚠ to cut them into thin slices (remove any seeds). ⚠ In a **food processor fitted with the metal blade attachment** ⚠ , *combine* the lemon slices, granulated sugar, and salt. Use the sharp knife ⚠ to cut the whole zested lemon you set aside earlier in half, and squeeze 2 tablespoons of lemon juice into the food processor bowl as well (remove any seeds). *Blend* for 1 to 2 minutes, until smooth. Set the food processor bowl aside.

7. **Cream the butter and eggs.** Place the softened butter in a **large mixing bowl**. Using a **handheld electric mixer** set to medium speed ⚠ , *cream* the butter for 1 minute. Add the cornstarch and *beat* for 30 seconds. Then, add the whole egg and egg yolks, one at a time, beating for 20 seconds after each addition. Use a **rubber spatula** to scrape down the sides of the bowl.

8. **Pour in the lemon mixture.** Add the lemon mixture to the butter mixture in 3 portions, and *beat* with the mixer for 20 seconds after each addition. Scrape down the sides of the bowl one more time, then beat for 20 to 30 seconds more, until smooth. Pour the filling into the cooled tart shell. With the tart still on its baking sheet, transfer it to the oven. ⚠

9. **Bake for 40 to 45 minutes.** The tart is done when the top is light golden brown but the filling is still slightly jiggly. Using the oven mitts, remove the baking sheet from the oven ⚠ and place it on the wire cooling rack to cool for 1 hour. Then, refrigerate for at least 2 hours.

10. **Remove the tart from the pan.** Take a small bowl (no wider than about 6 inches) and set it upside down on your countertop. Lift the tart pan with both hands* and set it on top of the bowl. Holding the tart pan steady, use both hands to gently pull the sides of the tart pan down until it falls off the pan onto the counter. Carefully transfer the tart to a **serving platter**. Slip a **large metal spatula** (the kind you'd use to flip pancakes) in between the tart and the bottom of the pan, and slide the tart off. Use the sharp knife ⚠ to slice the tart into wedges, and serve.

*Hold the tart pan from the sides, not the bottom. Remember, the pan is two separate pieces, so it can come apart.

Fresh 'n' Fruity Tart with Glitzy Glaze

Prep time:
1 hour 15 minutes

Bake time:
20 minutes

Cool time:
1 hour 30 minutes

Yield:
1 (*9-inch*) tart
(*8 to 10 servings*)

Ingredients

For the tart dough

7 tablespoons cold butter,
   plus 1 tablespoon softened*

1 lemon

1 cup all-purpose flour

¼ teaspoon salt

3 tablespoons brown sugar

1 large egg yolk*

1 tablespoon ice water

Nonstick cooking spray

*Turn to page 15 to learn
how to soften butter.
Use the same technique
to soften the cream cheese
in this recipe, too!

*Turn to page 14 to learn
how to separate eggs.

For the filling and fruit

½ cup (4 ounces) cream cheese, softened

4 tablespoons butter, softened

3 large egg yolks

¼ cup whole milk

¼ cup packed brown sugar

2 tablespoons cornstarch

2 teaspoons vanilla extract

1 cup heavy cream

2 tablespoons granulated sugar

2 cups colorful fruits (try berries, orange or kiwi slices, and pineapple chunks)

For the glitzy glaze

½ cup apricot jelly

2 tablespoons corn syrup

Instructions

1. **Preheat the oven to 375°F and prepare the tart pan.** Using your fingers, thoroughly *grease* a **9-inch tart pan** with the 1 tablespoon softened butter.

2. **Make the tart dough.** Using the smallest holes on a **box grater** (or a **Microplane zester** if you have one), *zest* the entire lemon into a **large mixing bowl.** ⚠ (Set the whole zested lemon aside for another use; you won't need it for this recipe.) Add the flour, salt, and brown sugar and *whisk* with a **fork.** Using a **butter knife**, cut the 7 tablespoons of cold butter into small cubes, and sprinkle them into the flour mixture. Using a **pastry blender or large fork**, *cut in the butter* with the flour mixture for about 5 minutes, until it looks rough and *shaggy*.

3. **Add the wet ingredients to the dough.** In a **small bowl**, *whisk* together the egg yolk and ice water with the fork. *Drizzle* it over the dough. Using the pastry

continues

blender or large fork, roughly mix for 30 seconds. Then, rub the mixture between your fingers for 1 minute or until it's mostly combined but still crumbly.

4. **Press the dough into the tart pan.** Transfer the dough to the prepared tart pan. Using your fingers, firmly press out the dough to evenly cover the bottom and go up the sides of the pan. Use the fork to *prick* the dough 20 to 30 times all over.

*Or use pie weights if you have them!

5. *Blind bake* the tart shell. Using **scissors**, cut out a circle of **parchment paper** that measures 12 inches across. Coat it lightly with nonstick cooking spray and place it over the tart dough, spray-side down. Pour 1½ cups uncooked rice or beans* on top of the parchment to weight down the dough. Place the tart pan on a **baking sheet** and transfer to the oven. ⚠ Bake for 20 minutes. Using **oven mitts**, remove the tart shell from the oven ⚠ and place it on a **wire cooling rack**. Carefully remove the parchment and rice or beans, and let the tart cool completely for 45 minutes while you continue the recipe. You can turn the oven off.

6. **Meanwhile, make the filling.** In a **medium mixing bowl**, *combine* the cream cheese and butter. Set the bowl aside. In a **separate medium mixing bowl**, use a **whisk** to *whisk* together the egg yolks, milk, brown sugar, cornstarch, and vanilla. Set this bowl aside, too.

7. *Temper* the egg mixture. In a **medium saucepan**, *combine* the heavy cream and granulated sugar. Set the pan over medium heat and let it warm up until the cream starts to *boil*, then remove the saucepan from the hot burner ⚠. Using a **ladle**, slowly *drizzle* the hot cream mixture into the egg mixture, *whisking* constantly with the whisk. Continue whisking until all the hot cream is incorporated, then pour the combined mixture back into the saucepan and place it over medium heat. ⚠

8. **Cook the filling.** *Whisking* constantly, bring the filling to a *boil* and cook for about 2 minutes until it has thickened. Remove the saucepan from the hot burner ⚠ and pour the filling over the cream cheese mixture.

9. **Blend the filling.** Using a **handheld electric mixer** set to medium speed ⚠, *beat* the filling for about 1 minute, until the cream cheese and butter are fully mixed in (the filling will be super smooth and creamy). Pour it into the cooled tart shell and spread it evenly with a **rubber spatula.** Let it cool completely for 30 minutes, then refrigerate for 1 hour.

10. **Meanwhile, prepare the fruit.** Wash and dry your fruits (and peel or trim them if necessary). Using a **sharp knife** ⚠, cut the fruit into bite-size pieces. Arrange the fruit on top of the cooled tart in any design you like.

11. **Make the glaze.** In a **small microwave-safe bowl**, *combine* the jelly and corn syrup. Microwave for 45 seconds, then stir with a **spoon**. Using a **pastry brush**, brush the mixture over the fruit, covering it entirely with warm glaze.

12. **Remove the tart from the pan.** Take a **small bowl** (no wider than about 6 inches) and set it upside down on your countertop. Lift the tart pan with both hands* and set it on top of the bowl. Holding the pan steady, use both hands to gently pull the sides of the tart pan down until it falls off the pan onto the counter. Carefully transfer the tart to a **serving platter**. Slip a **large metal spatula** (the kind you'd use to flip pancakes) in between the tart and the bottom of the pan, and slide the tart off. Cut the tart into slices with the sharp knife ⚠ and serve.

*Hold the tart pan from the sides, not the bottom. Remember, the pan is two separate pieces, so it can come apart.

Caramelized Banana Cream Pie

Prep time:
3 hours,
30 minutes

Bake time:
15 minutes

Cool time:
5 hours

Yield: 1 *(9-inch)*
pie *(8 to 10 servings)*

TEST
YOUR
SKILLS

Ingredients

For the dough

8 tablespoons cold butter,
   plus 1 tablespoon **softened***

1¼ cups all-purpose flour,
   plus more for rolling the dough

½ teaspoon salt

1 tablespoon brown sugar

1 teaspoon instant espresso

1 large egg yolk*

¼ cup ice water

Nonstick cooking spray

*Turn to page 15 to learn
how to soften butter.

*Turn to page 14 to learn
how to separate eggs.

Ingredients continued

For the caramelized bananas

6 bananas

1 tablespoon fresh lemon juice

2 tablespoons granulated sugar

2 tablespoons packed brown sugar

2 tablespoons butter

For the filling

2 tablespoons butter

⅔ cup store-bought caramel sauce

2 tablespoons granulated sugar

2 tablespoons packed brown sugar

⅓ cup all-purpose flour

2 cups whole milk

3 large egg yolks

½ cup heavy cream

½ teaspoon salt

1 tablespoon vanilla extract

For the caramel whipped cream

2 cups heavy cream

½ cup store-bought caramel sauce

Instructions

1. **Prepare the pie plate.** Using your fingers, thoroughly *grease* a **9-inch pie plate** with the 1 tablespoon softened butter.

2. **Make the pie dough.** In a **large mixing bowl**, *combine* the flour, salt, brown sugar, and instant espresso and *whisk* together with a **fork**. Using a **butter knife**, cut the 8 tablespoons cold butter into small cubes, and sprinkle them into the flour mixture. Using a **pastry blender or large fork**, *cut in the butter* with the flour mixture for about 5 minutes or until it looks rough and *shaggy*.

continues

3. **Add the wet ingredients to the dough.** In a **small bowl**, *whisk* together the egg yolk and ice water with the fork. *Drizzle* it over the dough. Using the pastry blender or large fork, roughly mix for 30 seconds. Then, rub the mixture between your fingers for 1 minute or until it's mostly combined but still crumbly. Form the dough into a ball and squash it down to form a disk. Wrap the disk tightly with **plastic wrap** and refrigerate for 1 hour while you continue the recipe.

4. **Meanwhile, caramelize the bananas.** Peel the bananas and use the butter knife to cut them into 1-inch slices, then place them in a **medium mixing bowl**. Add the lemon juice and *toss* the bananas to coat them, then set the bowl aside. In a **small bowl**, stir together the sugar and brown sugar with a **spoon**. Then, set a **12-inch skillet** on the stovetop and melt the butter over medium heat ⚠ . Add the bananas and cook for 5 minutes, stirring occasionally with a **heat-resistant spatula**. Sprinkle the sugar mixture over the bananas and continue to cook for 5 minutes more, until they're golden brown. Scoop the bananas back into the medium mixing bowl.

5. **Make the filling.** In the empty skillet, melt the butter over medium heat ⚠ . Using a **wooden spoon**, stir in the caramel sauce, granulated sugar, brown sugar, and flour. Cook for 3 minutes, stirring constantly and scraping up any leftover browned bits from the bananas. Slowly pour in 1 cup of milk, *whisking* to break up the flour mixture with a **whisk**. Pour in the remaining milk and whisk until smooth. Bring to a *simmer* and cook for 3 more minutes, then remove the skillet from the hot burner. ⚠

6. *Temper* **the egg mixture.** In a **large mixing bowl**, *whisk* together the egg yolks, cream, salt, and vanilla with the whisk. Using a **ladle**, slowly *drizzle* the hot milk mixture ⚠ into the egg yolk mixture, whisking constantly. Continue whisking until all the hot milk is incorporated. Then, *fold* in the cooked bananas with a **rubber spatula**. Set the bowl aside.

7. **Preheat the oven to 375°F and roll out the crust.** Clear off a clean surface and *dust* it lightly with flour. Place the dough disk on the floured counter. Sprinkle a

little more flour on top of the disk and rub some onto a **rolling pin.** Roll out the disk to form a circle that measures 12 inches across. Carefully wrap the dough around the rolling pin and transfer the dough to the prepared pie plate. Using your hands, gently press the dough down into the dish, smoothing to remove any trapped air bubbles. Use a pair of clean **scissors** to trim the edges of the dough, leaving 1 inch of dough to hang over all sides of the dish. Fold the overhanging dough under itself, then pinch to form a thick lip. *Crimp* the dough evenly around the edges with a **fork**. Then, use the fork to *prick* the bottom of the crust 20 to 30 times all over. Place the dish in the freezer for 15 minutes.

8. *Blind bake* **the crust.** Using **scissors**, cut out a circle of **parchment paper** that measures 12 inches across. Coat it lightly with nonstick cooking spray and place it into the bottom of the crust, spray-side down. Pour 1½ cups uncooked rice or beans* on top of the parchment to weight down the dough. Place the pie crust in the oven ⚠ and bake for 20 minutes. Using **oven mitts**, remove the crust from the oven ⚠ and place it on a **wire cooling rack.**
Leave the oven on, but reduce the oven temperature to 300°F. Carefully remove the parchment and rice, and allow the crust to cool for 30 minutes. Pour the filling into the cooled crust. Place the pie in the oven. ⚠

*Or use pie weights if you have them!

9. **Bake the pie for 15 minutes.** The pie is done when the filling is firm but still a little jiggly in the middle. Using the oven mitts, remove the pie from the oven ⚠ and place it on the wire cooling rack to cool completely for 1 hour. Then, refrigerate for a minimum of 4 hours.

10. **Make the caramel whipped cream.** Pour the cream into **a large mixing bowl.** Using a **handheld electric mixer** set to the highest speed ⚠ , *whip* the cream for 5 to 7 minutes. The cream should be very stiff. Pour in the caramel sauce and continue to whip for 20 seconds or until just combined. Spread the caramel whipped cream over the entire cooled pie, or cut the pie into slices with a **sharp knife** ⚠ and serve each piece with a generous *dollop* of caramel whipped cream.

Other Treats

Razzelberry Puffcakes with Sweetened Sour Cream

Prep time:
45 minutes

Bake time:
15 minutes

Cool time:
30 minutes

Yield:
12 puffcakes

Ingredients

For the puffcakes

Nonstick cooking spray

All-purpose flour, for rolling the dough

1 sheet (½ package) frozen puff
  pastry, thawed*

*Take the dough out of the
freezer 30 minutes before
you make this recipe!

For the filling

2 cups raspberries

½ cup granulated sugar

⅛ teaspoon salt

1 tablespoon fresh lemon juice

1 (¼-ounce) envelope unflavored gelatin

1 cup blueberries

1 cup strawberries

For the sweetened sour cream

1 cup sour cream

3 tablespoons powdered sugar

Instructions

1. **Preheat the oven to 400°F.** Turn a **12-cup muffin pan** upside down and coat the bottoms and sides of the cups with nonstick cooking spray.

2. **Prepare the puffcakes.** Clear off a clean surface and *dust* it lightly with flour. Unroll the sheet of puff pastry and lay it on the floured counter. Rub a little bit of flour on a **rolling pin** and roll the sheet out to form a square.✳ Using a **pizza wheel** ⚠ , make 2 vertical cuts and 3 horizontal cuts to form 12 equal-size rectangles of dough. Using your fingers, wrap a rectangle of pastry around the bottom of each muffin cup, pinching the sides together to form bowl shapes. Place a large sheet of **parchment paper** over the entire muffin pan, then place a **baking sheet** upside

✳Puff pastry sheets come in different sizes, depending on what brand you buy. You need it to be a square so you can cut out 12 evenly sized smaller rectangles. Try to roll the pastry into a square that is roughly 12 inches on all sides.

continues

down onto the parchment (this will help the dough hold its shape as it bakes). Place the whole thing in the oven. ⚠

3. **Bake the puffcakes for 15 minutes.** They're done when the pastry is golden brown and the sides are puffed. Using **oven mitts**, remove the pan from the oven ⚠ and remove the baking sheet and parchment. Let the puffcakes cool on the muffin pan for 30 minutes while you continue the recipe.

4. **Meanwhile, make the filling.** In a **medium microwave-safe bowl,** *combine* 1 cup of raspberries, the sugar, salt, and lemon juice and use a **fork** to mash together. Sprinkle in the gelatin and stir together with the fork, then let the mixture sit for 2 minutes. Microwave the mixture for 1½ minutes or until it's *boiling.* Use the oven mitts to remove the hot bowl ⚠ , and stir the mixture vigorously with a **spoon.** Transfer the mixture to a **large mixing bowl** and add the blueberries and the remaining 1 cup of raspberries. Using a **sharp knife** ⚠ and **cutting board,** cut the whole strawberries into small bite-size pieces, then add them to the berry mixture. Stir together with a **rubber spatula.**

5. **Make the sweetened sour cream and serve.** In a **small bowl,** *whisk* together the sour cream and powdered sugar with a **fork.** Arrange the pastry cups on **serving plates.** Spoon some fruit filling into each cup, and top with a *dollop* of whipped sour cream.

Baker's Notes

What went well? How can you improve next time?

RECIPE: ....

NOTES: ....

....

....

....

....

....

....

....

....

....

....

Dark Chocolate Truffles

Prep time:
25 minutes

Cool time:
4 hours,
10 minutes

Yield:
30 truffles

Ingredients

5 ounces **dark chocolate*** (in a bar, not chips)

1 tablespoon butter, softened*

½ cup heavy cream

1 tablespoon honey

½ cup unsweetened cocoa powder

*If you prefer milk chocolate
adjust the ratio of chocolate
to cream, using 6 ounces
of milk chocolate (a bar,
not chips) and ⅓ cup heavy
cream. Roll the truffles in
a mixture of ¼ cup pow-
dered sugar and ¼ cup
cocoa powder

*Turn to page 15 to learn
how to soften butter.

Instructions

1. **Chop the chocolate.** Using a **sharp knife** ⚠, chop the chocolate into very small pieces, and place them in a **medium mixing bowl.** Then, use the same knife to cut the butter into small pieces as well. Set the butter aside.

2. **Heat the cream and honey.** In a **small microwave-safe bowl**, *combine* the cream and honey. Microwave for 1½ minutes, making sure the mixture does not *boil* over. Using **oven mitts**, remove the hot bowl from the microwave ⚠ and pour the mixture over the chocolate. Let it sit for 1 minute while the chocolate melts.

3. **Whisk the cream into the chocolate.** Using a **whisk**, slowly stir the chocolate mixture in circles, starting from the center and working toward the outside of the bowl, until the mixture is super shiny and smooth. You've just created a ganache.*

   *Pronounced "guh-nosh," this is a mixture of melted chocolate and cream that's very common in baking.

4. **Stir the butter into the ganache.** Scatter the butter pieces over the ganache and *whisk* until they have completely melted. Pour the mixture into a **9-by-13-inch glass baking dish** and spread it out thinly and evenly with a **rubber spatula.** Let it sit at room temperature for 4 hours (or overnight) to *set*. Just before you're ready to roll the truffles, place the baking dish in the freezer for 10 minutes.

5. **Portion the truffles.** Drag a **melon baller or small spoon** across the top of the firm ganache in short strokes until it fills up (like scooping ice cream). Use your (clean) finger to push the portion of ganache to one side of the cold baking dish. Repeat until you've scooped all of the ganache into small portions.

6. **Finish the truffles.** Spread out the cocoa powder on a **large plate**; place **another large plate** nearby. Using your hands, pick up 1 chocolate portion and roll it between your palms for a few seconds to form a nice round ball. Drop it into the cocoa powder and roll it around until it's covered. Place the finished truffle on the clean plate. Repeat until all the truffles are finished.

Pumpkin Bread with Crumble Topping

Prep time:
30 minutes

Bake time:
1 hour 5 minutes

Cool time:
45 minutes

Yield:
One *(9-by-5-inch)*
loaf *(10 to 12 slices)*

Ingredients

For the crumble topping

¼ cup all-purpose flour

2 tablespoons brown sugar

⅛ teaspoon salt

⅛ teaspoon ground cinnamon

3 tablespoons butter, softened*

½ cup pepitas (hulled pumpkin seeds)

¼ cup mini chocolate chips

> *Turn to page 15 to learn
> how to soften butter.

For the pumpkin bread

Nonstick cooking spray

1¼ cups all-purpose flour

¼ teaspoon salt

½ teaspoon baking soda

¼ teaspoon baking powder

½ teaspoon ground cinnamon

½ teaspoon ground cloves

½ teaspoon ground nutmeg

½ teaspoon ground ginger

¾ cup (1½ sticks) butter, softened

½ cup packed brown sugar

½ cup granulated sugar

1 large egg

1 large **egg yolk** *

1 cup canned unsweetened pumpkin puree

¼ cup mini chocolate chips

*Turn to page 14 to learn how to separate eggs.

Instructions

1. **Make the crumble topping.** In a **small mixing bowl**, *whisk* together the flour, brown sugar, salt, and cinnamon with a **fork**. Using a **butter knife**, cut the butter into cubes, then scatter them over the flour mixture. Using a **large fork or pastry blender**, *cut in the butter* into the flour mixture until large clumps have formed. Sprinkle in the pepitas and chocolate chips and continue mixing until thoroughly combined. Set the bowl aside.

2. **Preheat the oven to 325°F and prepare the pan.** *Generously* spray a **9-by-5-inch loaf pan** with nonstick cooking spray and set it aside.

3. **Combine the dry ingredients for the pumpkin bread.** In a **medium mixing bowl**, *whisk* together the flour, salt, baking soda, baking powder, cinnamon, cloves, nutmeg, and ginger with the fork. Set the bowl aside.

continues

4. **Cream the butter and sugars.** In **a large mixing bowl**, *combine* the butter, brown sugar, and granulated sugar. Using a **handheld electric mixer** set to medium speed ⚠ , *cream* the butter and sugars together for 5 minutes, until it's light and fluffy.

5. **Add the wet ingredients.** Add the whole egg and egg yolk to the batter and *beat* for 1 minute. Add the canned pumpkin and mix for 30 seconds. Scrape down the sides of the bowl with a **rubber spatula** and beat for 10 seconds more.

6. **Add the dry ingredients.** Add the flour mixture to the butter mixture and gently *fold* with the rubber spatula until it is just combined, being careful not to over-mix. Add the chocolate chips and fold again to evenly mix them through the batter. Pour the batter into the prepared loaf pan, and smooth the top of the batter with the rubber spatula. Sprinkle the crumble topping over the batter and place the pan in the oven. ⚠

7. **Bake the bread for 60 to 65 minutes.** It's done when the topping is golden brown and the bread passes the **Toothpick Test** (see page 16). Using **oven mitts**, remove the bread from the oven ⚠ and place it on a **wire cooling rack** to cool in the pan for 45 minutes.

8. **Release the bread from the pan.** Gently run the butter knife along the inside edges of the pan. Then, flip the bread out onto a **cutting board** until it slides out of the pan. Turn the bread right-side up again, cut into slices, and serve!

Baker's Notes

What went well? How can you improve next time?

RECIPE: ....

NOTES: ....

....

....

....

....

....

....

....

....

....

....

Charlotte Russe with Raspberry Cream

Prep time:
45 minutes

Cool time:
4 hours

Yield:
4 to 6 servings

Ingredients

Nonstick cooking spray

12 to 15 store-bought ladyfingers

2 tablespoons ice water

1 (¼-ounce) envelope unflavored gelatin

1¼ cups raspberries, plus additional
  raspberries for *garnish*

2 teaspoons sugar

1 cup vanilla bean ice cream

1 tablespoon raspberry jam

¾ cup heavy cream

Powdered sugar, for *dusting*

Instructions

1. **Prepare the mold.** Coat the inside of a medium bowl* with nonstick cooking spray. Press the ladyfingers onto the sides of the bowl, standing them up vertically with their rounded sides touching the bowl and their flat sides facing inward.

2. **Soak the gelatin and macerate* the raspberries.** Place the ice water in a **small bowl** and sprinkle the gelatin over it. Set the bowl aside (the gelatin will absorb the water while you make the rest of the recipe). In a **separate small bowl**, *toss* the 1¼ cups raspberries with the sugar using a **large spoon**. Set this bowl aside as well.

3. **Heat the ice cream.** In a **small saucepan**, *combine* the ice cream and raspberry jam. Set over medium heat and warm, stirring constantly with a **whisk**, until the mixture is hot but not *boiling*. ⚠ Add the gelatin mixture and *whisk* until it completely dissolves. Remove the saucepan from the hot burner ⚠ and let the mixture cool for 15 minutes.

4. **Whip the cream.** Pour the heavy cream into a **large mixing bowl**. Using a **handheld electric mixer** set to the highest speed ⚠ , *whip* the cream for 5 minutes or until it forms stiff peaks.*

*The bowl you choose is important for this recipe! look for a deep bowl with a flat bottom and smooth, straight sides that can hold at least 4 cups of liquid.

*"Macerate" means to soften fruits by adding sugar, stirring, and allowing the mixture to rest while the fruits release their juices.

*The Beak Peaks Test (see page 16) can help you figure out whether your cream is whipped enough.

continues

5. **Add the whipped cream to the ice cream mixture.** *Sacrifice* one-third of the whipped cream into the cooled ice cream mixture in the saucepan and, using a **rubber spatula**, vigorously mix together. Pour the mixture back into the remaining whipped cream and *fold* gently with the rubber spatula until combined. Then, fold in half of the macerated raspberries.

6. **Fill the mold.** Spoon one-third of the raspberry cream into the bottom of the mold, taking care to keep the ladyfingers in place. Scatter half of the remaining macerated raspberries on top. Spoon on another one-third of the cream mixture, scatter the remaining berries over the cream mixture, and top with the rest of the cream mixture. Refrigerate for 4 hours to *set*.

7. **Unmold the charlotte russe.** Fill a **bowl that is larger than the mold** halfway full with hot water from the sink. Place the mold in the hot water, being careful not to get water in the dessert, and let it sit for 10 to 15 seconds. Place a **serving plate** upside down over the top of the mold, then carefully flip the whole thing over—the charlotte russe should release from the mold onto the plate. If it doesn't come out, flip the mold back over, place it back in the hot water for a few seconds longer, and then repeat the unmolding process.

8. **Serve!** *Garnish* with fresh raspberries and *dust* with powdered sugar.

Baker's Notes

What went well? How can you improve next time?

RECIPE: ....

NOTES: ....

....

....

....

....

....

....

....

....

....

....

....

Minty Grasshopper Trifle

Prep time:
45 minutes

Bake time:
18 minutes

Cool time:
30 minutes

Yield:
8 servings

Ingredients

For the chocolate mint sponge cake

Nonstick cooking spray

¾ cup all-purpose flour

2 tablespoons unsweetened
  cocoa powder

3 large eggs

¼ cup plus 2 tablespoons sugar

15 fresh mint leaves*

1 tablespoon butter

2 teaspoons mint extract

*Did you know there are
different types of mint? Bo[...]
the mint leaves and mint
extract should be spearmin[...]
not peppermint.

For the minty marshmallow cream

1½ cups heavy cream, plus 2 tablespoons

1 teaspoon green gel food coloring

2 cups marshmallow creme

2 teaspoons mint extract

For assembly

10 chocolate-covered chocolate mint
  cookies (such as Thin Mints)

2 or 3 fresh mint leaves, for *garnish*

Instructions

1. **Preheat the oven to 350°F and prepare the cake
    pan.** Coat an **8-inch cake pan** with nonstick cooking
    spray. Line the bottom with a circle* of **parchment
    paper**, then spray the parchment, too. Set the cake
    pan aside.

2. **Mix the dry ingredients for the cake.** In a **small
    bowl**, *whisk* together the flour and cocoa powder with
    a **fork**. Set the bowl aside.

3. **Whip the eggs and sugar.** In a **large mixing bowl**, *combine* the eggs and sugar.
    Fill a **medium pot** with hot water from the sink and place the bowl on top of it.
    Let the mixture warm for 5 minutes, then remove the bowl from the pot. Using a
    handheld electric mixer set to the highest speed ⚠ , *whip* the egg mixture for
    5 minutes or until it becomes very light in color and has tripled in volume.

*To make a parchment circle
that fits your pan perfectly,
place the cake pan right-side
up on top of the parchment,
trace around the pan with a
pencil, then cut the circle
$\frac{1}{4}$ inch smaller than the
circle you drew.

continues

4. **Finish mixing the cake batter.** Using a **sharp knife** ⚠, cut the mint leaves into very small pieces (you should have about 1 tablespoon of cut leaves). Add them to the batter and use the mixer to *blend* for 10 seconds. Pour in the flour mixture and gently *fold* with a **rubber spatula** until it's fully mixed. Place the butter in a **small microwave-safe bowl** and microwave for 30 seconds, until melted. Drizzle the melted butter and mint extract into the batter and fold again until it's combined. Pour the batter into the prepared cake pan, smooth the top with the rubber spatula, and place it in the oven. ⚠

5. **Bake the cake for 15 to 18 minutes.** It's done when it feels firm in the middle and passes the **Toothpick Test** (see page 16). Using **oven mitts**, remove the cake from the oven ⚠ and place the pan on a **wire cooling rack** to cool for 30 minutes while you continue the recipe.

6. **Begin making the minty marshmallow cream.** In a **medium saucepan**, *combine* the 2 tablespoons of heavy cream, the food coloring, and marshmallow creme. Set the pan over medium heat ⚠ and warm, stirring constantly with a **whisk** for 2 to 3 minutes, until the mixture is melted and liquidy but not hot. Remove the saucepan from the hot burner ⚠ and stir in the mint extract. Let the green marshmallow cream sit for 5 minutes.

*The Beak Peaks Test (see page 16) can help you figure out whether your cream is whipped enough.

7. **Make the whipped cream.** Pour the remaining 1½ cups of heavy cream into a **large mixing bowl**. Using the handheld electric mixer set to the highest speed ⚠, *whip* the cream for 5 minutes or until the cream holds stiff peaks.*

8. **Combine the two creams.** *Sacrifice* one-third of the whipped cream into the green marshmallow cream in the saucepan, and vigorously mix them together with a **heat-resistant spatula**. Pour this lightened marshmallow cream into the mixing bowl with the remaining whipped cream, and *fold* gently with the spatula until the minty cream is combined.

9. **Smash the cookies and tear the cake for assembling.** Place 7 of the cookies in a **resealable plastic bag**. Place the bag between **2 kitchen towels** and crush them into crumbs using a **rolling pin**. Use your fingers to break the remaining 3 cookies into quarters (12 pieces total). When the cake is cool, run a **butter knife** around the edges and tip the cake out of its pan onto the wire cooling rack. Use your hands to tear it into bite-size pieces.

10. **Layer the trifle.** Measure out 2 tablespoons of the cookie crumbs and set them aside in a **small bowl**. Place about one-third of the minty cream in a **large serving bowl**. Sprinkle with half of the cake pieces and cookie crumbs. Add another one-third of the minty cream, then the remaining half of the cake pieces and cookie crumbs. Top with the remaining minty cream and *garnish* with the reserved 2 tablespoons of cookie crumbs, the large cookie pieces, and whole fresh mint leaves and serve.

White Chocolate Crème Brûlée

Prep time:
30 minutes

Bake time:
37 minutes

Cool time:
4 hours 45 minutes

Yield: 6 (4-ounce)
ramekins

TEST YOUR SKIllS

Ingredients

2 teaspoons butter, softened*

6 large egg yolks*

1 teaspoon vanilla extract

⅛ teaspoon salt

1¾ cups heavy cream

¼ cup sour cream

¼ cup white chocolate chips

2 tablespoons sugar

*Turn to page 15 to learn
how to soften butter.

*Turn to page 14 to learn
how to separate eggs.

Crème brûlée (pronounced "krem broo-lay")
is a French dessert that means "burned
cream" in English. It's not actually burned,
though! The name refers to the caramelized
sugar crust on top.

Instructions

1. **Preheat the oven to 300°F and prepare the ramekins.** Before turning the oven on, adjust an oven rack to the middle position. Using your fingers, *grease* the insides of **6 (4-ounce) ramekins** with the butter and set aside.

2. **Whisk the egg yolks.** In a **medium mixing bowl**, *whisk* together the egg yolks, vanilla, and salt with a **fork**. Set the bowl aside.

3. **Heat the cream.** In a large **microwave-safe measuring cup** (the kind with a spout), *combine* the heavy cream and sour cream. Microwave for 2 to 3 minutes, until the cream is very hot, being careful not to let it *boil* over. Use **oven mitts** to remove the measuring cup from the microwave—it will be very hot! ⚠

4. **Melt the chocolate.** Place the white chocolate chips in a **separate medium mixing bowl** and pour the hot cream over them. Let the mixture sit for 1 minute while the chocolate melts. Then, *whisk* together with the fork until the chocolate is completely melted.

5. ***Temper* the egg yolks.** Use a **ladle** to slowly *drizzle* the warm chocolate cream into the egg yolk mixture, *whisking* constantly with a **whisk**. When it's completely combined, pour the mixture equally into the 6 prepared ramekins.

6. **Prepare a water bath.** Fill a **pitcher** with 6 to 8 cups of very hot water from the sink. Place the ramekins in a **roasting pan**. Using oven mitts, pull the middle oven rack out a little bit and place the roasting pan with the ramekins on it. ⚠ Gently pour the hot water from the pitcher into the roasting pan to create a *water bath*, being careful not to splash water into the ramekins. The water should come 1 inch up the sides of the ramekins.

continues

7. **Bake for 35 minutes.** The custards* are done when they feel firm. Using the oven mitts, remove the roasting pan from the oven. ⚠ (It will be heavy—ask for help!) Carefully remove the ramekins from the hot water (being careful not to get the oven mitts wet) and place them on a **wire cooling rack** for 45 minutes to cool completely. Place the cooled custards in the refrigerator for a minimum of 4 hours (or overnight) to completely *set*.

8. **Caramelize the sugar.** Adjust an oven rack to the highest position and turn the oven to the broil setting. Place the ramekins on a **baking sheet** and sprinkle them equally with the sugar. Place the ramekins in the oven. ⚠ Broil for about 2 minutes, until the sugar is brûléed (crunchy and caramelized). Using the oven mitts, remove the crème brûlées from the oven ⚠ and serve immediately. The top should make a *crack* sound when you break through it with a spoon!

Baker's Notes

What went well? How can you improve next time?

RECIPE: ....

NOTES: ....

....

....

....

....

....

....

....

....

....

....

....

....

Measurement Conversions

Volume Equivalents	U.S. Standard	U.S. Standard (ounces)	Metric (approximate)
Liquid	2 tablespoons	1 fl. oz.	30 mL
	¼ cup	2 fl. oz.	60 mL
	½ cup	4 fl. oz.	120 mL
	1 cup	8 fl. oz.	240 mL
	1½ cups	12 fl. oz.	355 mL
	2 cups or 1 pint	16 fl. oz.	475 mL
	4 cups or 1 quart	32 fl. oz.	1 L
	1 gallon	128 fl. oz.	4 L
Dry	⅛ teaspoon	–	0.5 mL
	¼ teaspoon	–	1 mL
	½ teaspoon	–	2 mL
	¾ teaspoon	–	4 mL
	1 teaspoon	–	5 mL
	1 tablespoon	–	15 mL
	¼ cup	–	59 mL
	⅓ cup	–	79 mL
	½ cup	–	118 mL
	⅔ cup	–	156 mL
	¾ cup	–	177 mL
	1 cup	–	235 mL
	2 cups or 1 pint	–	475 mL
	3 cups	–	700 mL
	4 cups or 1 quart	–	1 L
	½ gallon	–	2 L
	1 gallon	–	4 L

Oven Temperatures

Fahrenheit	Celsius (approximate)
250°F	120°C
300°F	150°C
325°F	165°C
350°F	180°C
375°F	190°C
400°F	200°C
425°F	220°C
450°F	230°C

Weight Equivalents

U.S. Standard	Metric (approximate)
½ ounce	15 g
1 ounce	30 g
2 ounces	60 g
4 ounces	115 g
8 ounces	225 g
12 ounces	340 g
16 ounces or 1 pound	455 g

Index

Acknowledgments

First and foremost, I'd like to thank my children (and the universe! *wink*) for reminding me, indirectly, to forever follow my dreams. I cannot begin to express how proud I am of you both. I hope someday to grow up and be just like you, minus the growing up part, of course! Then there's Charlie Brand, my very best friend, rock, and life support—thanks, dude! You're the best girlfriend-guy a girl could ever ask for! Also, this book only makes sense because of my fabulous editor, Reina Glenn—thanks for this wonderful opportunity and for translating my baking rants into helpful and useful information!

About the Author

Sarah Amorese is the creator of Piece, Love & Chocolate, an all-things-chocolate boutique and bakery in downtown Boulder, Colorado. In the spirit of lifelong learning and the joy of sharing her love of chocolate and baking with home chefs of all ages, she created Piece, Love & Chocolate University, an online community providing classes designed to teach skills and knowledge across the planet (going live January 2021). Sarah is the mother of two really great humans, a dog, and a small flock of chickens. She is also an artist, pastry chef, and chocolatier.

About the Illustrator

"Sweet" is the best way to describe **Enya Todd**'s illustrations. With a background in packaging design, Enya had a love of illustration that drove her toward painting food, particularly patisserie. Her smooth brushwork and soft palette perfectly capture the light-hearted finery of each delicious treat, while her enticing level of detail means you can almost taste what's in the picture. Now based in Bath, Enya is originally from Macau, though she has spent much of her career in London.

CPSIA information can be obtained
at www.ICGtesting.com
Printed in the USA
JSHW012051271120
9801JS00002B/2

9 781647 397814